THE AWA**KENING**

EXPERIENCE

The Awakening Experience

Promise Keepers

Reggie Dabbs

Thomas S. Fortson, PhD

Bishop Joseph L. Garlington, PhD

Erwin McManus

Buddy Owens

Bob Reccord, PhD

Dave Roever

Dan Seaborn

Greg Stier

Harold Velasquez

The Awakening Experience

Published as a cooperative effort between Promise Keepers, P.O. Box 103001, Denver, CO 80250-3001, www.promisekeepers.org; 1-800-888-7595; and Integrity Publishers, a division of Integrity Media, Inc., 5250 Virginia Way, Suite 110, Brentwood, TN 37027, www.integritypublishers.com.

Editorial Staff: Patty Crowley, Jennifer Stair, Stephanie Terry
Cover Design: Stoddard Design
Interior Design: Becky Hawley Design, Inc.

ISBN: 1-59145-377-1

Printed in the United States of America
05 06 07 08   9 8 7 6 5 4 3 2 1

And do this, understanding the present time. The hour has come for you to wake up from your slumber, because our salvation is nearer now than when we first believed.

—Romans 13:11

also available from promise keepers:

To order *The Awakening Worship* CD, or additional
The Awakening Experience books, call Promise Keepers at
1-800-888-7595 or go to www.promisekeepers.org

contents

introduction

And do this, understanding the present time. The hour has come for you to wake up from your slumber, because our salvation is nearer now than when we first believed. —Romans 13:11

Great, epic stories tap into our soul and make us yearn for a bigger reality and greater meaning in life. It's as if certain scriptwriters and film directors have a God-given talent to pull us out of our world and into the story's setting. The movie *Braveheart* tapped into many of our hearts and stirred a desire to die for a higher cause like freedom. Something in us relates to Frodo and Sam Wise Gamgee in *The Lord of the Rings* when their mission lured them to travel the dark mountains and caverns of Gondor, on a mission to defuse the evil power of Sauron. *The Matrix* drew us into Neo's decision between the red and blue pill. You see, something in our hearts longs to venture beyond the mundane of the status quo and to live connected to a higher purpose. Great stories rouse this urge.

There is a story of all stories, the largest and most real of them all—God's story. John Eldredge calls this God's "epic" reality in his book *Epic* (Thomas Nelson, 2004). Unlike fictional stories, written by people, God has authored this larger, ultimate reality.

Eldredge breaks God's epic story into five acts. Act 1 reveals God's hero heart, saturated with love and undefiled in the purity of the Trinity. Act 2 presents the antagonist, Satan, leading an uprising in heaven, luring other angels to question the good, loving heart of God. Act 3 introduces humanity's parents, Adam and Eve, into God's magnificently created earth, only to see the enemy entice them to question God's goodness and to betray their heavenly Father. God, in response, begins His pursuit of a straying humanity—including His pursuit of us. Act 4 introduces God's counterattack on the enemy in the birth, life, and death of His Son, Jesus Christ. Eldredge explains that God has gone to a great extent to win back His beloved—us! Act 5 is God's call and invitation to journey with Him, to come out of living in our smaller stories that are disconnected from His larger story and to align our hearts with the grand heart behind all that exists.

God has rescued us in Christ, set us free to follow Him, and now He invites us to live connected to the only story worth living in—*His story.*

It's Time to Wake Up!

If you were one of the tens of thousands of men who attended Promise Keepers' 2005 conference, The Awakening: An Unpredictable Adventure, then you will recall the theme verse for the conference, which is also the guiding verse for this book: "And do this, understanding the present time. The hour has come for you to wake up from your slumber, because our salvation is nearer now than when we first believed" (Romans 13:11).

Why do we need to wake up? Because we are a part of a larger, greater story, and there is a cosmic battle for our souls, hearts, and lives.

You will recall that you learned at The Awakening that an enemy does indeed exist; and though he is eternally defeated, this dark one is alive and well on earth. He is determined to rob your soul of eternal communion with God and to neutralize your heart and its effectiveness as long as you are alive on earth. An awakened man of God is a threat to the enemy's intentions to deceive, lure, and sedate human minds and souls with all his dark, deceptive tactics.

You will remember that you encountered at The Awakening the reality that the almighty God is also alive and present on earth . . . and He speaks to us, strengthening and leading us through this broken and battle-torn world. You learned that He longs to engage your thinking, living, and relating in very tangible and real ways,

Our life on earth becomes our life journey —our story.

guiding you into territories on earth that expand His kingdom in other human hearts. You learned that your identity is firmly rooted in Christ and that your Father in heaven proudly declares that you are His son. You are God's *son*; and no one, not even the dark enemy, can steal this reality from you.

You also learned that God created you with a life purpose, vision, and mission that are intricately connected to His grand, epic story. Your Creator has known you from the day your father's twenty-three chromosomes combined with your mother's twenty-three chromosomes to make forty-six—a combination of forty-six characteristics like no other combination in human history. From that moment in time, God designed your personality, natural talents, physical attributes—everything about you—with purpose and intention.

That is the incredible miracle of life: one life with a unique design, an eternal vision, and a purpose for living for a specific point in time. Our life on earth becomes our life journey—our story. Whether our life story is connected to God's epic story depends on our relationship to our Creator, His unique design and purpose for us, and our willingness to live the life He created us to live.

Stop and Contemplate

But few men suspend their activities long enough in our fast-paced culture to contemplate their design, their life purpose, and the implications for who they are and what they should do with the time God grants them on earth. How often have you heard of deathbed regrets? Too much time spent pursuing more money or the job of a lifetime. Not enough time invested in relationships with people they love and who love them.

Have you ever punched the pause button on your life in order to contemplate why you are alive? This pause must be long enough for you to understand—and embrace—God's vision and purpose for your existence with all the implications for how you should live it.

Few of us have done so.

Consider for a moment how a human life is summed up just three generations removed. When you recall the name of one of your great-grandfathers, what two or three words sum up his life? Was he a kind man? Loyal? Godly? Abusive? Generous? Grumpy? An alcoholic? A leader? Did he actively love your great-grandmother?

Most likely, you never met your great-grandfather in person, but your grandparents and parents may have relayed his legacy to you. It's fascinating, isn't it? Just three generations removed, and a man's life is summed up in just a few words.

What if you could script the two or three words that your great-grandchildren will hear about your life? What words would you pick? These kinds of questions pull us out of our current matrix of life and challenge us to contemplate our life purpose and meaning on earth.

Recall David in the Bible. He's known for his courage against Goliath, his rise from a shepherd and musician to a warrior and king, his adultery with Bathsheba and murder of Uriah, and as a man after God's heart. Acts 13:36 sums up his life on earth in one sentence: "When David had served God's purpose in his own generation, he fell asleep." What a compelling life legacy! With all his life experiences, fears, courageous living, mistakes, and flaws, David served the purpose of God in his own generation.

Do you sense your heart's desire to serve God's purpose for your generation?

We all sense this desire if we pause long enough to listen to it. It's a desire that God Himself places in us. But let's be honest: life is hard. We struggle. We fail. We feel trapped in life's currents. The fast tides of work and family pull us out to sea. At times, we get sucked into undercurrents of darkness and brokenness. But at some point in our life journey, we reflect on the purpose of life: *Why am I here on earth? Who am I? What is my purpose in human history?*

To penetrate the core of these issues, we need to ask the right questions, get brutally honest, hear God's thoughts, and connect

But let's be honest: life is hard. We struggle. We fail.

with a few friends in safe and authentic relationships. This road of discovery and insight is a journey, and adventures unfold.

Chart Your Life Map

When we travel, we typically use a map to guide the journey. A map keeps the journey on course even when unpredictable events and surprises intercept the quest. Likewise, in life, we need a life map. Think about this for a minute. The Bible is clear that God creates each person uniquely (see Psalm 139:13–16). Each person is distinct in his or her composition; the blend of natural talents, spiritual gifts, personality, life experiences, and passions for life make each person a one-of-a-kind individual in human history.

Proverbs 15:21 says, "The empty-headed treat life as a plaything; the perceptive grasp its meaning and make a go of it" (MSG). God creates each of us to love and fear Him, be a part of His family, and grow in Christlikeness. But few of us know what this means for our unique design. We need a life map to guide our journey and help us discover the applications of what these truths mean for us individually.

Charting your life map takes time. It is a *process*. Most likely, you will not chart your life map overnight. It will unfold. God will use others to help you make discoveries; and with the work of His Spirit, He will help you gain insight into your life path so that you can serve His purposes for your generation in your lifetime.

Everyone leaves a legacy—for good or bad. Few men consider their life legacy long before they die and leave it. It is possible for you to tap into God's unique design and its implications for all areas of your life: your personal life, home life, work life, church life, community life, and friendsships. But it doesn't just happen. A life lived with intention and alignment to God's design and vision for that life is a process of discovery, focus, alignment, and adventure.

The Awakening Experience Process

Everything in life is accomplished through some kind of process. Manufacturers create product through production processes. War-torn nations rebuild their infrastructure through civic and political processes. God created the heavens and earth through a seven-day process. Ecosystems thrive and die through biological processes. Churches plan weekly services and outreaches through processes.

Our spiritual growth also is a process.

Conversion stories abound in which a person is rescued from the depths of darkness and brought into the kingdom of God. Scripture is clear that there is a future and present reality to a man's spiritual conversion. Hebrews 10:14 says, "For by one offering He has perfected forever those who are being sanctified" (NKJV). The future declares that God now sees us eternally united with His Son, our Lord and Savior Jesus Christ, covering our lives with His once-and-for-all sacrifice for our sin and His eternal righteousness. The present reminds us that we must now become who we already are in Christ. The present life of growing in Christlikeness is called sanctification.

And sanctification is a *process*.

This book was conceived during the planning of The Awakening conferences because Promise Keepers' leadership understands that Christlike change and living is a process. Real spirituality is not prescriptive. You cannot just swallow a few spiritual pills every day to root out sin and live a life of peace, safety, and meaning. It just doesn't work that way, and we all know it. In this adventure of life, unexpected tragedies, illnesses, dangers, and unpredictable twists and turns affect us at any given point in time.

But the man who has learned to hear the voice of his Father and to focus his life to serve God's purpose for his life on earth is an awakened man who will go anywhere and do anything for God and His kingdom. To the enemy, he is a dangerous man. To the Father,

> Scripture is clear that there is a future and present reality to a man's spiritual conversion.

he is a servant and son whose talents, treasures, and time on earth will help him accomplish his eternal purpose.

This workbook is built around a process—the Awakening Experience Process—that will guide you to design a life map that is unique to God's life purpose for you. If you attended The Awakening conference, then you are aware that this process is designed for you to progress in the context of relationship—with a few other men and/or your wife. There is no time line on this process. Take as much time as you need to hear from God, gain clarity, and get clear on His purpose and adventure for you.

As the following table illustrates, the Awakening Experience Process guides you through four phases:

1. **Awareness**—Awakening to Who I Am
2. **Focus**—Awakening to God's Life Adventure for Me
3. **Preparation**—Awakening to How I Must Live
4. **Freedom**—Living the Awakened Life

The Awakening Experience Process

Phase 1 **AWARENESS** *Awakening to Who I Am*	Phase 2 **FOCUS** *Awakening to God's Adventure for Me*	Phase 3 **PREPARATION** *Awakening to How I Must Live*	Phase 4 **FREEDOM** *Living the Awakened Life*
My Life in Christ Taking Inventory My Heart My Life Story My Giftedness	My Life Purpose My Life Vision My Life Mission The Primary Obstacles in My Path	My Guiding Convictions Personal Battle Plan Family Battle Plan Work Battle Plan Church Battle Plan Community Battle Plan	Friendship Battle Plan Guides Along the Way Time Analysis Life Journey Reviews
Where Am I Now?	Where Does God Want to Take Me?	How Must I Live to Get There?	How Will I Stay the Course?

You may be aware of the Seven Promises of a Promise Keeper. Since they were introduced in 1993, some have viewed them prescriptively, or legalistically, and assumed that if they make the commitment to keep the Seven Promises, then they will indeed keep them. But we all know that this is not the way life works. We make promises with good intentions; but because of our humanness, we fail to various degrees. We learn over time that we need God's help even to make a promise, let alone keep it. This is why God loves a humble heart!

The Awakening Experience Process will serve as a road map or guide to help you keep the promises that God has called you to keep. Note in the following table how the Seven Promises are really about relationships: your relationship with God and yourself, your relationship with your family and friends, your relationship with your local church and church-at-large, and your relationship with your community, including your work community, neighborhood, and global community.

We learn over time that we need God's help even to make a promise, let alone keep it.

The Seven Promises		Relationships Targeted in the Promise
1	A Promise Keeper is committed to honoring Jesus Christ through worship, prayer, and obedience to God's Word in the power of the Holy Spirit.	A man's relationship with God
2	A Promise Keeper is committed to pursuing vital relationships with a few other men, understanding that he needs brothers to help him keep his promises.	A man's relationship with his friends
3	A Promise Keeper is committed to practicing spiritual, moral, ethical, and sexual purity.	A man's relationship with himself
4	A Promise Keeper is committed to building strong marriages and families through love, protection, and biblical values.	A man's relationship with his family
5	A Promise Keeper is committed to supporting the mission of his church by honoring and praying for his pastor and by actively giving his time and resources.	A man's relationship with his local church
6	A Promise Keeper is committed to reaching beyond any racial and denominational barriers to demonstrate the power of biblical unity.	A man's relationship with the church-at-large
7	A Promise Keeper is committed to influencing his world, being obedient to the Great Commandment (see Mark 12:30–31) and the Great Commission (see Matthew 28:19–20).	A man's relationship with his community (work, neighborhood, global community)

Consequently, we have designed the Awakening Experience Process to help you in these relationships, combining the relational categories inherent in the Seven Promises into six:

1. Your Personal Life (Promises 1 and 3): This category includes your relationship with God and yourself, including issues of integrity, care for your physical body, emotional health, and personal interests that maintain health and balance.

2. Your Home Life (Promise 4): This category includes those relationships in your home. If you are married and have kids, obviously it includes your wife and children. If not, then you may have roommates or other living scenarios. Adjust this category to your circumstances.

3. Your Work Life (Promise 7): This category includes your relationships with co-workers (peers, boss, those who report to you, clients and customers, and so on).

4. Your Church Life (Promises 5 and 6): This category includes your life in your local church and your relationship to the extended body of Christ, the church-at-large. Specifically, it includes your pastor and/or leadership team and others you relate with on various levels.

5. Your Community Life (Promise 7): This category is your world apart from your community of faith. It may include your immediate neighborhood or the global community. Customize this category to target your unique situation.

6. Your Friendships (Promise 2): This category includes those friends who know you deeply and walk through life with you.

When you have completed the Awakening Experience Process, you will have the following tools to help you live a life awakened to God's purpose for you with customized applications to your unique scenarios. You will have:

- An understanding of your life journey, unique gifts, and composition
- An understanding of what God has written on your heart and tools to help you hear His voice and move forward
- Clarity on your life purpose, vision, and mission
- Battle plans for each of the six relational categories listed above: your personal life, home life, work life, church life, community life, and friendships

You will have the ...tools to help you live a life awakened to God's purpose for you.

- Strategies to help you journey with a few close friends and assess your progress as you live the awakened life in Christ

Messengers of the Awakening Experience Process

Promise Keepers for years has benefited from the talent and skill of God's messengers, men who have offered their skill of communication to speak to men's hearts and give them a vision for living a life after the ultimate Man of all men: Jesus Christ. This workbook is no different. Each chapter is written by a Promise Keepers conference speaker who will inspire your thinking and heart on selected subjects. We thank Dave Roever, Buddy Owens, Reggie Dabbs, Bishop Joseph Garlington, Dan Seaborn, Dr. Bob Reccord, Erwin McManus, Greg Stier, and Dr. Tom Fortson. Each of these men has written his chapter with a passion for the message and a desire to stir your thinking and heart. After each chapter, components of the Awakening Experience Process follow and guide you to discover, develop, and live a life that is awakened to God's purpose for you on earth.

We also want to acknowledge and honor a man who many in the business world have deemed "the best process thinker alive." His name is Tom Paterson. The idea of developing an awakening process for The Awakening conferences in 2005 was, in part, inspired by Tom's LifePlan process from his book *Living the Life You Were Meant to Live* (Thomas Nelson, 1998). For decades, Tom has facilitated and trained facilitators of one-on-one LifePlans. Though the Awakening Experience Process is not the LifePlan process, and though Tom did not personally develop these awakening tools, we acknowledge and honor Tom's influence in our thinking. For those interested in learning more about the LifePlan process, we encourage you to obtain a copy of *Living the Life You Were Meant to Live*.

Components of the Awakening Experience Process

Before you embark on the awakening journey, consider some critical components of the adventure:

• **A few other men:** We can discover great depths about ourselves alone. But we can go so much deeper when we engage life with others. The Awakening Experience Process is designed for you to journey through with a few comrades. Are there at least two men you can approach and ask if they would be willing to take this adventure with you? It's risky, but the rate of honest discovery and follow-through exponentially increases when life is lived in real, authentic relationships with a few other men who desire the same clarity and focus in life.

• **Cover each other:** As you gather with these men, discuss and agree on the ground rules for your time together. You will discover things about yourself and each other that may be dark and very personal. Proverbs 17:9 says, "He who covers over an offense promotes love, but whoever repeats the matter separates close friends." When you get to know your friends, you may offend each other and learn of one another's struggles and humanness. Agree at the beginning of this process to cover each other with love and confidentiality. If one of you takes the risk to offer the group the gift of his confession, understand that it is a gift that he gives to you. For you to give that gift to someone else, without his permission (even to your wife!) is sin—the sin of gossip. And in doing so, you will separate yourself from your friend. Nothing shuts down the work of God in a man's life and becomes a tool of the enemy more effectively than gossip that exposes another man's private confessions. So if something is shared in your group that is clearly designed to stay in your group, keep it in the group! Cover him with grace, confidentiality, and forgiveness. Don't let the enemy use you to expose your friend to others and thwart God's work in his life. If the enemy has us pinned down in some way, we need

The goal is not speed but depth of discovery and clarity.

at least one safe friend with whom we bring the dark stuff into the light—without the fear of exposure, condemnation, or the response to fix things. Be that friend.

• **Get real:** Deep authenticity is nurtured in safety and mutual openness. When one man takes the risk of opening up the caverns of his life and heart to another, but the other man stays shallow, the man who opened up will most likely not take the risk to open his life to that depth again. This is a basic principle of disclosure. So ask each other if you are willing to get deep and real with one another as safety and trust grows. Now we shouldn't go around being fully transparent to everyone. That is simply not wise. But we should be fully known to a few fellow comrades in the battle of life. Ultimately, we should have this kind of depth of relating with our spouse, but some men need counsel and help in getting to this point with their wife. We may need to open up first to another friend. But if you do so in your group, all need to be committed to the same depth of sharing life.

• **Go for depth of discovery, not speed:** Unlike typical study guides that tell you how much to study per gathering and how often to gather, the Awakening Experience Process in this book is designed for you to set your own pace and time line. You can download all of the awakening tools at our web site **www.promisekeepers.org/AwakeningExperience** in order to customize them, edit them, print them out, and keep them active and useable in your computer and day-planner systems. With that said, find a time and place to meet regularly. Some of you might meet every week and get through the process in ten weeks. Some of you may take an entire year. You may spend an hour on some of the awakening tools and months on others. The goal is not speed but depth of discovery and clarity. The intent in this process is to connect with God, hear from Him, invite your friends into your Awakening Experience Process, and let God use them as sounding boards. In time, you will gain clarity on your purpose in life so that you can live awakened and alert as you move forward. So don't rush the process! Go for depth of discovery, and help each other tap into God's heart for each.

Use the Awakening Experience Process to lay out God's design of who you are and His unique call on your life with all its applications to the adventure before you. And in the end, God can declare of you and your fellow journeyers what He said about David: "When (insert your name) had served God's purpose in his own generation, he fell asleep." What a way to live! Go for it!

—The Promise Keepers Creative Team
Harold Velasquez
Jeff Rasor
Chantell Hinkle
Pete Richardson

God can declare of you and your fellow journeyers what He said about David.

the battle for a man's soul

Dave Roever

I fought two wars, both of them in Vietnam. One was a military war that brought serious physical injury and a lifetime of recovery. The second war was a spiritual war battling for my soul—a war that brought isolation, rejection, and the potential of seriously breaking the hearts of those I love. Both had bona fide risks and lifelong challenges to my mind and body beyond what words can describe.

Fighting the Physical War

The military war was America's epic confrontation of communism in Vietnam. This ten-year conflict was the longest, bloodiest, and most misundersood war in American history. Demonstrations and debates went to the extreme, with American antiwar activists protesting the troops who fought to defend the very ideals that allowed these activists the right to protest in the first place. Soldiers like myself questioned whether we wanted to return to America only to have our fellow citizens throw bottles of paint and urine at us. Thousands of miles away, we were fully aware of the battle for political ideals that was raging in our homeland.

I grew up in a minister's home. It was a haven of peace and nonviolence. I never had a black eye in my youth, yet I found myself serving in the Brown Water Black Beret, a special warfare unit of the U.S. Navy, fighting in the jungles of Vietnam.

My experience in Vietnam turned up close and personal very quickly when I realized that the burning flesh I smelled July 26, 1969, was my own. Nearly half the skin on my body and most of my face burned that day. The white phosphorus grenade exploded about six inches from my right ear and damaged my body. I will never fully recover. I watched skin melt from my hands and arms. I could even see my heart beating in my chest. My face had literally dissolved onto my boots. The explosion blinded my right eye and destroyed the hearing in my right ear. The pain was so intense that my brain does not recall the sensation. To this day, I cannot find the words in any language to describe what I felt that day.

I spent one year and two months in the hospital at Brooke Army Medical Center in San Antonio, Texas. I was released with a body disfigured by war and scarred for life. I continue to fight the battle to survive these war injuries. But these scars are physical and on the outside.

Fighting the Spiritual War

The second war I fought in Vietnam was spiritual and on the inside. People do not typically consider this war important. Like the physical war, I fought this spiritual war with all my heart and soul. The outcome of this war would mean the difference between life and death when I returned home, though I am sure I did not fully understand the truth of this statement at the time. The decisions I was making on a daily basis were bound to affect the rest of my life: drugs or no drugs, liquor or no liquor, sexual sin or no sexual sin. I faced all of these choices, not on a one-time basis, but daily.

These choices were never easy. Everyone in my special boat team unit scrutinized each of my decisions. Opportunities to indulge in sexually deviant movies were frequent. Booze orgies were common. Because I would not participate, I was often isolated and on the outside of comradeship. I longed for a friend. I missed my wife, Brenda, the love of my life; and the fellowship of the church folks at home. I wanted someone to pray for me. Chaplains did not visit us, and without Christian relationships I struggled to keep the faith. I had to stand alone and brace myself each time I took a position with Christ.

Has a figurative hand grenade exploded in your life?

Each member of my immediate boat team had a nickname for me. One called me "Dudley Do-Right." Another labeled me "Dr. Do-Little." The third mocked me as "Preacher Man." I, in turn, responded by calling them "Pervert Number One," "Pervert Number Two," and "Pervert Number Three." That's how we got along: the Preacher Man and the Perverts. It sounds like a gospel band, doesn't it?

This spiritual war was much more than name-calling and exclusion. As in the physical war, I was completely at the mercy of the training I received prior to combat. The physical war's training was extreme, demanding, and essential to my survival. Likewise, my spiritual war training from my father was essential for my spiritual survival. He taught me with instruction and example, living his life as a foundation of ethics, character, and morality upon which I could build my life.

These two wars battled in epic proportions for my body and soul.

The Battle for Our Souls

I cannot possibly know the battles you have fought or may even now be fighting. Has a figurative hand grenade exploded in your life? For most of us, it is a grenade exploding in our soul . . . our inner man. The battle being fought there is spiritual and reflects the cosmic, epic battle between God's kingdom and Satan's. This battle is beyond our physical sight. It's as if a thin veil cloaks our vision so that we see through it darkly.

But make no mistake: we do sense this battle for our soul! Even with limited access, visually impaired by the finite, we know that this war is fought not by flesh and blood, but by angelic spiritual beings intricately engaging human activity on earth—for good or evil. In the Bible, we learn that one-third of God's angelic hosts were excommunicated from heaven with Lucifer, or Satan. That means that two-thirds are on your side! That's two-to-one in your favor. However, you have the deciding vote. If your vote is for evil, then the battle for your soul is up for grabs!

You are the deciding factor in the cosmic battle for the soul. Each of us has our own unique battles. The sniper's bullet or the grenade thrown at you comes in many forms: divorce, drugs, hatred, habits, anger, apathy, lust . . . you name it. And the wounds that the enemy inflicts on your soul are fatal without spiritual healing and deliverance from a supernatural source.

I am deeply aware that the devil invades our lives only "to steal and kill and destroy" (John 10:10). When the grenade exploded in my face and blew off nearly half my skin, I was left wounded, but not dead. This spiritual enemy of my soul took aim, lowered the boom, and took his best shot. He hit me, knocked me halfway into eternity, threw down his stick, and walked off laughing . . . and I'm still here!

I had a choice to make. I could lie there and burn and bleed, crying because the enemy of my soul hurt me and beat me with a stick of injury until I was a bloody pulp . . . and just give up and die. Or I could use that same stick to help me get back on my feet, shake it in the devil's face, and tell him, "Get back here! This war is not over!" By God's grace and with His power, I took that stick and am battling the enemy wherever God instructs me to go.

People of every nation in every part of the world fight this spiritual war, whether they are aware of it or not. It's no different for us in America. Sadly, millions of men have had no spiritual training for the battles of our times, and the enemy wreaks destruction in our souls using weapons like pornography, drug and alcohol addiction, financial mismanagement, and family breakups. Too often, these men are humiliated with the exposure of their hidden sin. With their wounded souls scarred from spiritual war injuries, it's as if they have no hope for wholeness and healing. Their wounds are on the inside!

When a man faces these internal wounds, hidden in darkness and ignored for years, he opens up his soul for a spiritual awakening. The battle for the soul is fierce. The enemy uses the vices and habits of our sinful inclinations to keep us from discovering

I am who I am because Jesus Christ has won the battle for my soul!

and surrendering to the only One who can rescue and heal us. But when a man gets brutally honest with himself, confronts his past, and acknowledges his need for help, that is when God unleashes His presence and resources to heal his soul and to create wholeness from his brokenness.

If you are at this point of desperation and desire spiritual healing, your wounds become your path to God. What do you do with them? You cry out to your Father in heaven, ask Him to forgive your sin, and declare Jesus Christ as Savior and Leader. When you do this, God forgives your sin through the sacrificial death of Jesus Christ on the cross, gives you the free gift of Christ's righteousness, and sets you on a path of freedom in Christ and healing from your spiritual wounds. When you do this, you are in essence using the enemy's stick against him—you are taking your past, acknowledging your forgiveness in Christ, and no longer hiding in shame and guilt.

The devil used a stick against Jesus—a stick in the form of a cross. Jesus is using that very stick against the devil at this moment to fight for your soul—a battle that simply demands your vote in favor of Christ. The deciding vote is yours. Make that decision today, even now. Simply ask Jesus into your life and confess your sins; He will deliver you and set you free!

Wounds That Bring God Glory

On September 11, 2001, I watched in utter horror as Islamic fanatics flew aircrafts filled with innocent people into buildings filled with innocent people. I stood in my hotel room, slamming my fist into my hand and vowing I would not be left out of this war. God heard my prayer, and the military invited me to Iraq and Afghanistan, as well as to every other country in the Middle East where our troops are risking their lives.

They didn't call me because of my good looks or my academic achievements. (I was in the top 10 percent of the lower one-third of my graduating class.) Their stated reason for inviting me was that I had survived military war, and I carry the physical scars from injuries inflicted in battle. Soldiers, they said, would relate to me. But I believe that the real reason they invited me supersedes my scarred face and mutilated body. They called because I am more than a conqueror through Christ (see Romans 8:37). I am who I am because Jesus Christ has won the battle for my soul!

People often ask if I would enlist to fight the physical war again, knowing that I might lose more body parts or become further disfigured and scarred. This question always disarms me. What I learned fighting the physical war taught me to fight the spiritual war at a greater level. My time in Vietnam is a vital chapter to my life story. Though physical wounds have altered my appearance, my scars now exist to bring glory to God.

I like to think of my life as a glove filled by God's hand. Whether I am holding a dying soldier in Iraq as he slips away into eternity or addressing an audience with a message of hope and healing, I can finally and honestly say to God, "My wounds have been worth it to bring glory to You, and if required or requested, I will do it again and again and again . . ."

I like to think of my life as a glove filled by God's hand.

THE AWAKENING EXPERIENCE PROCESS

phase 1: awareness

My Life in Christ

Dave Roever just encouraged you to trust your life to Jesus Christ. Perhaps you have never done so. Maybe you have. Either way, when a man confronts his own human condition and the reality and nature of his Creator—his Father in heaven—his life takes the most dramatic turn of his existence. If you have never admitted your sin to God, acknowledged your need for His help, and confessed Jesus Christ as your Lord and Savior, then read the following pages written to help you understand the foundation and reason for this life-altering decision.

Man-to-Man About Being a Son of God   (Romans 8:14–15)

A man's relationship with his father is basic. The benefit of a strong, affirming bond with Dad is powerful. On the other hand, the pain of a lost or nonexistent relationship with an earthly father can last a lifetime. Insecurity and crippled relationships with others are often traced back to the deficiencies from an unloving, unaccepting father.

God Loves His Sons   (John 3:16)

God's love is strong, fatherly, and complete. Men from all over the country are beginning to understand this relationship for the very first time. Many have spent years trying to gain God's approval through some sort of performance—that is, doing good things. But it is impossible to live like God's sons before we have a relationship with Him. The problem is that we are born into a world that is separated from this kind of intimacy with our Maker. It is as if a wall of separation has come between God and humanity; and so instead of a relationship with God, we discover a barrier. But there is good news!

Reconciliation Is Possible Through Christ (2 Corinthians 5:18)

God has made it possible to have a close, personal relationship with Him. Reconciliation is now possible. If you do not have a personal relationship with God that is like that of a son with his dad, then this is your primary need. Consider these questions:

- If God made me, then why do I need to be reconciled with Him?
- What happened to my relationship with God that needs repairing?
- If I choose to reject this relationship with God, what are the consequences?

The following paragraphs address these and other questions you may have. As you read, understand that the invitation to have a personal relationship with God applies to the religious or nonreligious. So if there is distance between you and God and you do not yet know His acceptance, then contemplate the following words with an open mind and heart.

We Lost a Relationship (Romans 3:23)

Adam, the father of the human race, made a terrible choice. We are born into the aftermath of his failure. The mess began with Adam's act of disobedience. He willingly joined his wife in doubting God's word and ignoring his instructions. They decided not to trust God's goodness and promise. In doing so, they distanced themselves from God's presence and His original desires for them.

Consequently, the close, personal relationship between mankind and God was severed. Additionally, Adam failed Eve, his wife, in the process of disobeying God; and from that point forward, contention entered into their relationship. His relationship with his sons went from bad to worse. One of his sons even killed the other one (see Genesis 2–4). We could even say that Adam later lost his job and was kicked off the family farm. Pain, sweat, and difficulty now

In our relationship with God, we just can't fix the endemic problem.

flavored his labor. Bottom line: Adam's life fell apart once he drifted from God.

It's no different for us today. We inherited a diseased spiritual DNA when we were conceived, so we shouldn't be surprised to experience failure and sin in our lives. As a result, our choices continue to create distance between us and God. So what our souls long for—a personal relationship with our Creator—is out of reach. The chasm is wide. The distance is too real.

The New Testament describes this dilemma as being "separate from Christ . . . without hope and without God in the world" (Ephesians 2:12). Just as parents teach their kids that all actions have consequences, so it is with our quandary with God. If we die alienated from God, we will experience the horrible reality of eternal separation from Him!

What We Need: A Restored Relationship   (John 17:20–21)

Jesus Christ is the only one able to restore the relationship we have lost with God. Because our spirits are tainted with sin, they need a new beginning—a new life. God has made it possible through the life, death, and resurrection of Jesus Christ to bring new life to us spiritually and to restore our relationship with God our Father.

The only requirement for us in this spiritual transaction is for us to receive. For many of us men, this is an obstacle because we are by nature driven to fix things ourselves. But we can't fix this spiritual problem. To begin, then, we have to admit that we're far from perfect, that we do in fact mess up and are sinners. In doing so, we declare that we need help and open the door for God to help us.

You see, when we do it our way, we remain isolated in our sin. We separate ourselves not only from God but also from right relationships with our families and others. In our relationship with God, we just can't fix the endemic problem. Until we come to terms with this reality, the distance from God will remain.

How Can the Relationship Be Restored?   (Ephesians 2:8–9)

Why do we need Jesus Christ? First, God has to respond to our inclination to sin. If His response was directly toward us, we could not withstand the consequences for our sin. God's solution, then, was to send His Son, Jesus Christ, to earth in the form of a man. Christ was born without sin and did not sin in His lifetime. He willingly took upon Himself the penalty, or judgment, for our sin and allowed Roman soldiers to crucify Him on a cross. In doing so, He paid the price for our sin so we wouldn't have to.

On His cross, Jesus removed the barrier that our sin constructed. When we comprehend what Christ's life and death offers us, we realize why it's not enough for us just to decide to do a little better. We need help—God's help—and He has given us that help in Christ. "For it is by grace you have been saved, through faith—and this not from yourselves, it is the gift of God—not by works so that no one can boast" (Ephesians 2:8–9).

This is what a lot of men miss! A relationship with God is a gift. We don't earn it. We can't buy it. We can't boast or feel a sense of accomplishment about achieving it. It is given out of love—God's love extended to us.

> A relationship with God is a gift. We don't earn it. We can't buy it.

A Gift Must Be Received   (John 1:12)

The only thing that can keep a man from accepting this free, spiritual gift of restored relationship with God is pride. What about you? Do you see your need for God? Can you receive this gift of eternal life through Jesus Christ? If you can receive it, God makes a promise to you. He says, "Yet to all who received him, to those who believed in his name, he gave the right to become children of God—children born not of natural descent, nor of human decision or a husband's will, but born of God" (John 1:12–13).

If you would like to accept this gift of eternal life and restored relationship with God, Jesus Christ has secured it for you. All you need to do is ask God to save you from the consequences of your sin. Your belief and trust in Him saves you, because you admit your need for His help.

Following, you will find a prayer similar to the one that the men at Promise Keepers prayed during The Awakening conference. Perhaps you have never personally prayed this kind of prayer. Or perhaps you prayed it years ago and have drifted from God. Or perhaps you prayed it years ago, and reading it stirs up memories and thankfulness for how God rescued you from darkness and the jaws of the enemy, forgave your sin, and declared you to be His eternal son.

Whatever your reference is to this prayer of confession of sin and faith, reread it and use the blank page that follows the prayer to write a letter to your Father in heaven—a letter that expresses your gratitude to God for restoring your relationship with Him, your desire to entrust your life to Him today, and your desire to follow Him from this day forward.

A Prayer to Accept or Reaffirm Your Acceptance of Christ

Father, I've come home. Please make me Your son. I turn from my sin. I accept Your forgiveness, made possible through Jesus Christ by His death and resurrection. I place my faith and trust in Jesus Christ alone. I receive Him as my Savior and Lord. I want to follow and serve You. Thank You for battling for my soul and awakening it to Your love and purpose for my life. Let today be the beginning of my new journey as Your son and a member of Your family. You have always kept Your promises. Help me to keep my promises too. In Jesus's name, I pray. Amen.

a letter of gratitude and commitment

Today's Date: _____

Dear Father,

Your son,

phase 1: awareness

Accurate perspective primes our brains and hearts for breakthrough thinking and future planning. Insight gained into current realities in our life opens us to hear from God and embrace His vision and desires for us. Perspective, like growth in Christ, is a process. At some point in this process, it's as if the lights go on and we enter a clearer awareness of who we are and are not.

Remember, the Awakening Experience Process is a journey. Phase 1 is the "awareness" stage. In this phase of the process, you will be guided through several exercises, each one serving as a tool to help you gain perspective and awareness of the man God created you to be and what he created you for. You just wrote a letter to God, thanking Him for the gift of eternal life and restored relationship with Him. Next, you are going to reflect on a series of questions designed to help you take honest inventory of your life at this point in time. Below, you can see where we are in the Awakening Experience Process.

The Awakening Experience Process

Phase 1 **AWARENESS** *Awakening to Who I Am*	Phase 2 **FOCUS** *Awakening to God's Adventure for Me*	Phase 3 **PREPARATION** *Awakening to How I Must Live*	Phase 4 **FREEDOM** *Living the Awakened Life*
My Life in Christ ***Taking Inventory*** My Heart My Life Story My Giftedness	My Life Purpose My Life Vision My Life Mission The Primary Obstacles in My Path	My Guiding Convictions Personal Battle Plan Family Battle Plan Work Battle Plan Church Battle Plan Community Battle Plan	Friendship Battle Plan Guides Along The Way Time Analysis Life Journey Reviews
Where Am I Now?	Where Does God Want to Take Me?	How Must I Live to Get There?	How Will I Stay the Course?

The right questions at the right time can prompt honest reflection and help us see what previously blinded us. Consider just a few timely, strategic questions God asked individuals in Scripture:

- Genesis 3:9: "Where are you?" (God to Adam)
- Genesis 4:9: "Where is your brother Abel?" (God to Cain)
- Genesis 16:8: "Where have you come from, and where are you going?" (The angel of the Lord to Hagar)
- Luke 8:25: "Where is your faith?" (Jesus to the disciples after the storm at sea)
- John 13:12: "Do you understand what I have done for you?" (Jesus to the disciples after washing their feet)
- John 18:21: "Why question me?" (Jesus to Annas, the high priest)
- Luke 6:32: "If you love those who love you, what credit is that to you?" (Jesus to the disciples)

Sincere questions require frank, honest answers. As you begin the Awakening Experience Process, you enter an adventure that will stir your heart and mind as to the man God created you to be and what He is asking and desiring for you to do—now and in your future. You may need to find an uninterrupted place that is conducive to reflection as you get real and honest with yourself and with God.

The following tool is a list of questions designed to help you do this. You will be asked a series of questions targeted to different spheres of your life: your personal life, home life, work life, church life, community life, and friendships. These questions are designed to incite reflection and stir up discovery. This is between you and God and perhaps a few close friends who can give you feedback and help you probe deeper, if necessary.

Note in the following awakening tools, you are asked to reflect on the questions in the left-hand column and assess where you are awake, in a slumber, and asleep. What do these questions mean?

These questions are designed to incite reflection and stir up discovery.

- **If you are awake:** This part of your life is going well. Things are right. You are "hitting on all cylinders" or "living in your zone." You are satisfied with the level of your alertness to your desires, goals, and dreams in this area of your life. For example, you may be in a healthy place spiritually—satisfied with your level of connection to God and learning the joy of walking with Him fully surrendered. Or you may be awake to your needs for physical health and discovering the habits and rhythms for health.

- **If you are in a slumber:** Some areas of your life are not clear, not where you desire. It's as if you are neither fully awake nor completely tuned out. You are in the stage in between full alertness and sleep. You're not seeing things clearly, and you need clarity. For example, you may be bored and burned out with life in general and not know why. Or you might feel that your marriage has been stale for some time and you do not understand why you feel this way. Or you might be confused about how you can use your talents and gifts in your church.

- **If you are asleep:** Some things are just not right, and you know it. But you are ignoring these things. It's as if you have a blind spot to these issues. It's not a slumber, because it's blatantly wrong. You're not confused about what's wrong; in fact, the issue is clearly wrong and needs attention, but you have ignored it or denied it. It's as if you are sleepwalking in these areas of your life. For example, one of your kids might desperately need your attention and focus, and it's time to reconnect. Your marriage might be in red-alert status, and you've been ignoring this reality. Or you are aware of how the spiritual enemy has sabotaged a relationship with a friend or neighbor, and it's time to awaken to this reality and move toward reconciliation. You may ask, how can a sleeping man know if he is asleep? Good question. That is why we need friends and our wife to help us identify these "asleep" issues in our life. Allow them to probe and prod into your heart and life, restrain from defending yourself, commit to listening and learning what you may not see, and set the course of your heart to grow toward awakening in these areas.

• **If you are comatose:** You may be more than asleep in some areas of your life. Comatose issues are in red-alert status—in the intensive care unit. For example, your marriage may be near breakup and you may not know it (or you do know it, but you are in denial). Again, you will need your friends and/or wife to help you discern and identify any issues in your life that fall into this comatose category.

After you have reflected deeply and honestly in the different spheres of your life, summarize in the right-hand column the priority issues that need your attention. These are the highlight insights that you gleaned from the process of identifying where you are awake, in a slumber, asleep, or comatose. These primary issues will help you later in the awakening process when you develop battle plans for each area of your life.

Note that an example is offered for the personal life inventory. Throughout the Awakening Experience Process, a fictional example is presented of a man going through the Awakening Experience Process, to help you see how the tools work.

Comatose
issues are
in red-alert
status—in
the intensive
care unit.

Personal Life Awakening Assessment Tool

Statements to Stir Reflection	My Current State of Awakening				Priority Issues
	Where Am I Awake?	Where Am I in a Slumber?	Where Am I Asleep?	Where Am I Comatose?	

Personal Life

My Spiritual Heart
- My heart is fully free in Christ and free from dark, sinful obsessions.
- I have a healthy relationship with God and hear His voice regularly.
- I know the nature of the enemy of my soul and am learning how to fight him effectively.
- I am fully surrendered to God.
- I know God's life calling and purpose for me and am moving in that direction.

My Physical Body
- I believe my body is a living temple of God's presence.
- I take care of my body with appropriate exercise, nutrition, and sleep.

Personal Life Awakening Assessment Tool

My Current State of Awakening

Statements to Stir Reflection	Where Am I Awake?	Where Am I in a Slumber?	Where Am I Asleep?	Where Am I Comatose?	Priority Issues
My Mental/Emotional Health • I have discovered healthy outlets to keep "my emotional tank" full and maintain good perspective in life. • I understand whom God has uniquely created me to be and what to do and am learning to live in this zone.					
My Sexual Life • I am learning how the enemy tempts me with the dark side of sex and am learning to battle accordingly. • I am learning how to express my sexuality in healthy ways. • I am open and honest with a few others about my sexuality.					
My Finances • I am learning to steward the finances God has given me. • I am learning to get out and stay out of debt.					

Personal Life

Personal Life Awakening Assessment Tool ➤ Fictional Example

Personal Life

Statements to Stir Reflection	My Current State of Awakening				Priority Issues
	Where Am I Awake?	Where Am I in a Slumber?	Where Am I Asleep?	Where Am I Comatose?	
My Spiritual Heart • My heart is fully free in Christ and free from dark, sinful obsessions. • I have a healthy relationship with God and hear His voice regularly. • I know the nature of the enemy of my soul and am learning how to fight him effectively. • I am fully surrendered to God. • I know God's life calling and purpose for me and am moving in that direction.	• I have committed my life to Christ. I know He has forgiven me and continues to forgive me of my sin. Where would I be if He had not rescued me from my sexual sin and the abortion that I helped facilitate? Where would I be without my relationship with Him?	• My heart has tasted real spiritual freedom at times, but I know that my heart needs more healing and that there is more for me to realize in the area of true spiritual freedom. • I'm not hearing God's voice as I have in the past. I need to take time out of my hectic-paced life and connect with Him.	• I don't really know how to fight the enemy in the area of my sexuality. It seems that I usually feel guilty for thinking about things I shouldn't or yielding to sexual temptation. Lauren, my wife, is threatened by this reality in me as a man. I'm ashamed to really get real with my friends. What if they tell others? What should I do with this?	• I am not in touch with healthy inputs into my life. When I relax, I feel guilty. I feel that I spend most of my time at work. The time I have left I give to my family. I don't really know what a healthy personal life feels like at this stage in my life. How do I walk with God with everything else I have going on in my life?	1. I need to reconnect with God and hear from Him. 2. I need to learn how to fight the enemy's tactics and temptations. I have never learned how to do so.
My Physical Body • I believe my body is a living temple of God's presence. • I take care of my body with appropriate exercise, nutrition, and sleep.					

Personal Life Awakening Assessment Tool ▶ Fictional Example, cont.

My Current State of Awakening

Statements to Stir Reflection	Where Am I Awake?	Where Am I in a Slumber?	Where Am I Asleep?	Where Am I Comatose?	Priority Issues
My Mental/Emotional Health					
• I have discovered healthy outlets to keep "my emotional tank" full and maintain good perspective in life.					
• I understand whom God has uniquely created me to be and what to do and am learning to live in this zone.		• I know some of my unique talents and gifts, but I am not really clear about my uniqueness and life purpose.			3. Of all the areas of my life, my personal life is the most fragile and neglected. I need help and encouragement in this area.
My Sexual Life					
• I am learning how the enemy tempts me with the dark side of sex and am learning to battle accordingly.					
• I am learning how to express my sexuality in healthy ways.					
• I am open and honest with a few others about my sexuality.					
My Finances					
• I am learning to steward the finances God has given me.	• I take care of my/our finances diligently. This is one area of my life that I monitor closely and have a good sense of stewardship over.				
• I am learning to get out and stay out of debt.					

Personal Life

Home Life Awakening Assessment Tool

Statements to Stir Reflection	My Current State of Awakening				Priority Issues
	Where Am I Awake?	Where Am I in a Slumber?	Where Am I Asleep?	Where Am I Comatose?	
Home Life					
My Spouse (if married) or Girlfriend (if dating)					
• I am learning the unique design of my wife and how to encourage her in her life journey.					
• I am learning to open up my life and heart to my wife.					
• I am learning how to forgive and be forgiven on a regular basis.					
• I am learning to make sacrifices to express my love to her.					
My Children (if a father)					
• I understand my role as a dad.					
• I am learning my kids' unique designs and how to encourage them to be all that God created them to be.					
• I am learning the value of spending time with my kids and how to creatively pursue their lives and hearts.					

Home Life

Statements to Stir Reflection	My Current State of Awakening				Priority Issues
	Where Am I Awake?	Where Am I in a Slumber?	Where Am I Asleep?	Where Am I Comatose?	

My Parents
- To the best of my ability, I have a healthy relationship with my parents and in-laws (if applicable).
- I have forgiven them for any wounds I experienced from them in my past.
- I have appropriately "left" my parents and "cleaved" to my wife (if married).

My Extended Family
- I do my best to encourage my siblings and other extended family.
- I'm aware of the issues that threaten the unity of our extended family and pray and take appropriate action toward unity.

Work Life Awakening Assessment Tool

My Current State of Awakening

Statements to Stir Reflection	Where Am I Awake?	Where Am I in a Slumber?	Where Am I Asleep?	Where Am I Comatose?	Priority Issues
Work Life					
My Present Vocation • I am in my "zone" vocationally. • I understand my core talents and am optimizing them at work. • I believe that God has placed me in my present workplace and know how He wants to use me in the lives of my co-workers.					
My Supervisor • I have a healthy relationship with my boss. • I honor my boss in what I say and how I work. • I understand how God wants to use me in my boss's life.					
My Peers • I understand that my faith is expressed not only in what I say at work, but in how I make decisions, how hard I work, the skill of my work, and how I treat other people.					

Work Life

Statements to Stir Reflection	My Current State of Awakening				Priority Issues
	Where Am I Awake?	Where Am I in a Slumber?	Where Am I Asleep?	Where Am I Comatose?	
My Employees/Staff					
• I encourage and build them up to become all that they can be.					
• When they fail, I engage them and help them grow as a result of it.					
• I communicate well to my staff and do not leave them wondering what I am thinking in regard to them.					
• I am learning to run/block for my staff.					
Our Customers					
• I treat people with respect and honesty.					
• I do not sacrifice my ethical values in dealing with customers and clients.					
• I believe God has me in their lives for a reason.					

Church Life Awakening Assessment Tool

Church Life

Statements to Stir Reflection	My Current State of Awakening				Priority Issues
	Where Am I Awake?	Where Am I in a Slumber?	Where Am I Asleep?	Where Am I Comatose?	
My Relationships					
• To the best of my ability, I attempt to nurture honest, healthy, reconciled relationships among my church family.					
• I have pursued any unreconciled relationships and have done all that I can to be at peace with everyone in my church.					
• I honor and respect my pastors and church leadership and do not talk behind their backs.					
• I pray for my church leadership regularly: for them to hear God clearly, to follow Him boldly, and to be protected from the enemy's attacks.					

Church Life

Statements to Stir Reflection	My Current State of Awakening				Priority Issues
	Where Am I Awake?	Where Am I in a Slumber?	Where Am I Asleep?	Where Am I Comatose?	

My Gifts

- I know my spiritual gifts and talents and understand how to use them in my church family so that others benefit from them.

- I understand that my money is not mine but God's, and I regularly practice the habit of giving a percentage of my income back to God's church.

- I am learning how to honor God's purposes by investing my time, talent, and treasures in His kingdom through my church.

Community Life Awakening Assessment Tool

Community Life

Statements to Stir Reflection	My Current State of Awakening				Priority Issues
	Where Am I Awake?	Where Am I in a Slumber?	Where Am I Asleep?	Where Am I Comatose?	
Awareness • I am becoming more aware of whom God has placed in the community of my life. • I am learning to pray for those God has put in my life and to be more alert to what He is doing in their lives.					
My Neighborhood • I am learning the names of my neighbors, praying about how I can connect with them, and am open to God's showing me how to be His agent in their lives.					

Community Life Awakening Assessment Tool

Statements to Stir Reflection	My Current State of Awakening				Priority Issues
	Where Am I Awake?	Where Am I in a Slumber?	Where Am I Asleep?	Where Am I Comatose?	
Community Life					
My Community-at-Large • I understand that God wants to use who I am and what he has done in my life to love others and to tell the story of my life. • I am learning to strategically get involved in my community with the intention to meet new people and be a presence of love, hope, encouragement, and health in my community. • I am open to serve God's purposes in other cultures different from mine, either in my own country or another one.					

Friendship Awakening Assessment Tool

Friendships

Statements to Stir Reflection	My Current State of Awakening				Priority Issues
	Where Am I Awake?	Where Am I in a Slumber?	Where Am I Asleep?	Where Am I Comatose?	
Authenticity • I have a few close, spiritual friends who know me deeply. They are safe, and I consider them close brothers in Christ. • I am a safe friend to my friends. They know that I will receive their confessions with full confidentiality, cover them with grace, and under no condition share their confession with anyone else unless they give me permission to do so.					

Friendships

Statements to Stir Reflection

Encouragement

- My friends and I are learning one another's unique designs and how we can stir each other up to be all God created us to be.

- I am learning to pour courage into my friends' lives by being an encouragement to them.

- I understand that my friends are on a journey as I am and that we need each other to fulfill God's vision and purpose for each of us.

My Current State of Awakening

Where Am I Awake?	Where Am I in a Slumber?	Where Am I Asleep?	Where Am I Comatose?	Priority Issues

checkup

Throughout the Awakening Experience Process, we will take timely checkups of our progress. By now, you have written a letter to your Father in heaven expressing gratitude and heart-to-heart communication about your freedom in Christ, His unique design and purpose for you, and your commitment to live the awakened and free life.

You have also taken a comprehensive inventory on the current realities in your personal life, home life, work life, church life, community life, and friendships. How are you doing so far? Has this been easy, or has it been difficult? Are you letting others into the process with you?

Remember, this is a process. There are no right and wrong answers. This is a journey of the heart toward awakened living. Fight the enemy's message to hide, to preserve the secret life. When we pursue the awakened life to live in the light of Christ, the enemy is threatened. Stay open and honest with your friends who journey with you.

The awakening adventure now takes us into the battle for your heart. Harold Velasquez will stir your thinking and reflecting as he opens his own heart. The enemy in the epic story is after your heart. He knows if he silences or neutralizes your spiritual heart, then you will not live the life God made for you.

So dig in. Help each other stay in the battle and in the process of allowing God to awaken you to the abundant life He has for you.

Onward!

the battle for a man's heart

Harold Velasquez

I stood on the side of the platform, serving on the staff of Promise Keepers, when Stephen Newby, our worship leader, suddenly called me stage front. The worship had been personal and intimate. God was working in the hearts of men in a real and powerful way. For some reason, Stephen sensed that I had something to say. I wasn't so sure.

As I walked to speak to thousands of men, I asked God for the words to say, and the events of the last few months began to flash through my mind. I struggled because I didn't want to have to share my failure as a father with these guys. How could I? I'm a vice president for Promise Keepers. I'm supposed to be an example of what a godly man looks like. But I knew the truth, and God was asking me to get real about my life at that moment. I spoke, and the words flowed. Opening up my heart in this way at that time was one of the most challenging events of my life.

I have three daughters. Each one is beautiful and special to me. I vividly remember the gratitude I felt when they were born and recall praying something like this: "Lord, help me to raise them to follow after You, that they'll never fall to the temptation of drugs, alcohol, or sex outside of marriage, that they'll follow after You all of the days of their lives." Just two months before Stephen's invitation for me to join him on the Promise Keepers' platform, my unmarried middle daughter had informed my wife and me that she was pregnant. We were shocked. I can't begin to describe the pain, the hurt, and the disappointment—not to mention the incredible anger that rose up within me. I wanted to hurt somebody. I wanted to strike back.

At that moment, the stakes were high. The real battle was in my heart. It always is, and Satan was on the offensive. I began to doubt myself. I felt like a failure as a father, a mentor, and a spiritual leader. How could I lead other men? How could I teach other men? How could I work in a men's ministry when I felt so ineffective in leading my family? I began to question everything about myself as Satan bombarded the dreams and visions that God had written on my heart.

I'm convinced that this is one of the enemy's most effective methods to derail us from living the life God wants us to live. When Satan is able to lure a man's heart into the prison of failure and self-doubt, he effectively neutralizes that man's effectiveness in ministry. When my daughter delivered the news of her pregnancy, the battle in my heart raged.

War in Our Hearts

In the opening scene of *First Knight*, Lancelot badgers a carnival-like crowd to sword-fight him for money. He had progressively outdu-eled all contenders, ending each challenge with a quick flick of his weapon that dismantled his opponent's sword and sent it high into the air, and then catching it with his free hand before it landed. Lancelot ended each victory with a bow.

A tall, blond, and thick-boned young man named Mark stepped into the dueling circle for his chance to de-sword Lancelot. The crowd hushed. Mark split an upright log with his iron sword to dis-play his strength. The crowd was awed, and the sword-fight ensued. Mark stood his ground and even showed signs of possible victory. But then the inevitable happened: Lancelot maneuvered his sword into a silver flurry, sending Mark's weapon head over tip into the air. Lancelot caught it, and the crowd applauded.

Alone with Lancelot afterward, Mark asked, "How did you do that? Was that a trick?"

"No. No trick. It's a way of fighting."

"Tell me. I can learn," pleaded Mark.

"You have to study your opponent—how he moves, so you know

This side of death we can expect this spiritual battle never to let up.

what he's going to do before he does it," said Lancelot, staring into Mark's eyes.

"I can do that," responded Mark.

"You have to know that one moment in every fight when you win or lose. And you have to know how to wait for it."

"I can do that," repeated Mark.

"And you have to not care whether you live or die," said Lancelot.

Mark was silent.

The enemy of our lives is after our hearts. This battle is spiritual. It is ongoing. This side of death we can expect this spiritual battle never to let up. So if we are going to have any chance to fight it effectively, we need to know the nature of the enemy of our hearts, grow in anticipating his next move, and battle with a mind-set that we don't care whether we live or die.

Our hearts are under siege, battled, wounded, and war-torn. But few men are aware of this reality. In his bestseller *Wild at Heart*, John Eldredge calls this battle for our hearts exactly what it is—an all-out war.

We are now in the late stages of the long and vicious war against the human heart. I know—it sounds overly dramatic. I almost didn't use the term "war" at all, for fear of being dismissed at this point as one more in the group of "Chicken Littles," Christians who run around trying to get everybody worked up over some imaginary fear in order to advance their political or economic or theological cause. But I am not hawking fear at all; I am speaking honestly about the nature of what is unfolding around us . . . against us. And until we call the situation what it is, we will not know what to do about it. In fact, this is where many people feel abandoned or betrayed by God. They thought that becoming a Christian would somehow end their troubles, or at least reduce them considerably. No one ever told them they were being moved to the front lines, and they seem genuinely shocked at the fact that they've been shot at.[1]

I appreciate John Eldredge's writing about the heart, because he helps us understand that because of this war over our hearts, our hearts are wounded to various degrees. As a result, in the case of my daughter's pregnancy, the enemy neutralized a young man from living the adventure God wrote on his heart, numbed him to this heart battle, and quieted his pursuit to capture the beauty of his woman.

The battle for our hearts is real.

A New Heart, a New Adventure

For years, I was made to believe that it was not only dangerous to live from the heart but that this thinking was contrary to the Scriptures. The heart untouched by God is, as Jeremiah declares, "deceitful above all things, and desperately wicked: who can know it?" (Jeremiah 17:9 KJV). Consequently, I was taught to ignore my heart, to silence it, and certainly not to live from it.

But Scripture has much more to say about our hearts. Do you know that Christ came to free our hearts? "Christ has set us free to live a free life. So take your stand! Never again let anyone put a harness of slavery on you. . . . It is absolutely clear that God has called you to a free life. Just make sure that you don't use this freedom as an excuse to do whatever you want to do and destroy your freedom. Rather, use your freedom to serve one another in love; that's how freedom grows" (Galatians 5:1, 13 MSG).

This Christ-freed heart is a spiritual heart, given to us by God and foreseen by Ezekiel: "I'll remove the stone heart from your body and replace it with a heart that's God-willed" (Ezekiel 36:26 MSG). God promised, in His new covenant in Christ, that we would experience a heart transplant—our stony hearts replaced with new, pliable hearts.

I was given a new heart and made a new creation at the tender age of ten. At that time, my parents had been separated on and off

This Christ-freed heart is a spiritual heart, given to us by God.

for almost four years. My brothers and I were living with my mom on welfare. Even then, I felt like all my hopes and dreams had been crushed by my parents' separation. I thought that I would never amount to anything and that the bad things happening to my family were my own fault.

When Christ entered my life and gave me a new heart, He made me into a "new creation" (2 Corinthians 5:17). Not only were my hopes and dreams restored, but God also filled my heart with faith for my future. I began to believe God for the impossible. I prayed for two things: (1) that God would allow me the privilege of sharing with the world the hope that I'd found in Christ, and (2) that God would bring my parents back together again. He answered both prayers. My parents reconciled within six months; and within a year, I was recording Christian music and sharing my testimony nationwide. It was the beginning of my own unpredictable adventure—walking by faith, not by sight. Though I cannot anticipate all the variables of my future, I have learned that God's faithfulness is a constant in this journey of life.

It doesn't take long to discover that, while we will experience glorious victories in serving Christ, we are engaged in a relentless battle as long as we're in this world. And it is a battle for the heart: your heart, the hearts of your loved ones, and the hearts of the people around you. When my daughter informed me of her pregnancy, she was in need of her daddy's love—a love that would awaken her to God's grace, mercy, and love in the same way I had experienced it in my journey. I knew this. I also knew that if I would ever experience healing in my heart, I would need to forgive the young man. I cannot tell you how I struggled forgiving him. But I began asking God to help me see the baby's father as God saw him. All I could pray was, "Lord, I know You love him with unconditional love. Would You love him through me?" God helped me to see that this young man was not my enemy, and my daughter was not my enemy.

I'm learning that this war is different from human conflicts. It's a spiritual war. Paul said in 2 Corinthians 10:3–4, "For though we live in the world, we do not wage war as the world does. The weapons we fight with are not the weapons of the world. On the contrary, they have divine power to demolish strongholds." With our new, spiritual hearts, we have access to spiritual weapons, in Christ, to battle the spiritual enemy. But to do so, we have to learn how to fight this spiritual war with spiritual weapons.

Living from the New Heart

This spiritual war is anything but predictable. I've been awakened to the fact that the enemy does all he can to dishearten us. He uses bankruptcy, divorce, abuse, apathy, layoffs, unexpected pregnancies, sickness, death, boredom, and many other life circumstances to cause us to lose heart. Oftentimes, we sabotage our own hearts with bad habits or poor choices. I know this firsthand. I've lost count of how many times I've blown it—situations when I made the wrong choice. I've watched enticing things on television that filled my mind with things I later regretted. I've retaliated out of self-defense and pride, blurting hurtful words to those I care about. Yet I've encountered God's loving grace every time I sin.

If we're honest, we all struggle. We do things we don't really want to do. The new heart I received when I became a believer wants to follow Christ, but the flesh with its own desires opposes God and is self-driven. I've learned that my old nature is intent on indulging fleshly impulses and drives me to perform and look good to others.

Romans 7:18–21 summarizes what I've learned about myself: "I realize that I don't have what it takes. I can will it, but I can't *do* it. I decide to do good, but I don't *really* do it; I decide not to do bad, but then I do it anyway. My decisions, such as they are, don't result in actions. Something has gone wrong deep within me and gets the better of me every time. It happens so regularly that it's predictable. The moment I decide to do good, sin is there to trip me up" (MSG). Add Satan and the culture's ability to incite my old nature to sin, and

Oftentimes, we sabotage our own hearts with bad habits or poor choices.

it's easy to say with Paul: "I've tried everything and nothing helps. I'm at the end of my rope. Is there no one who can do anything for me? Isn't that the real question?" (Romans 7:24 MSG).

Hope for the Heart

Satan does all he can to stir our fleshly heart and its dark desires. Too often we feed our old heart by succumbing to distractions, isolation, or vice. Over time, we can easily forget and silence the dreams God has written on our heart. If we don't understand this battle, the intent of the enemy, and how to fight, we can easily lose heart altogether and settle for the mundane, unadventurous, and unchallenged life full of apathy and complacency.

While I may have lost many battles along the way, I can say with full assurance that I've not lost the war. As Paul said in 2 Corinthians 4:8–9: "We've been surrounded and battered by troubles, but we're not demoralized; we're not sure what to do, but we know that God knows what to do; we've been spiritually terrorized, but God hasn't left our side; we've been thrown down, but we haven't broken" (MSG). Solomon said in Proverbs 24:16: "A righteous man falls seven times, and rises again. But the wicked stumble in time of calamity" (NASB). How can a man be righteous if he falls? The answer is that with God's help, he gets back up.

You see, followers of Christ are in process while on this earth. This process is called sanctification. Hebrews 10:14 says, "By one offering He has perfected forever those who are being sanctified" (NKJV). This process started the day we confessed Jesus Christ as the Lord of our lives. He continues helping us mature spiritually through His Holy Spirit. "Is there no one who can do anything for me?" asked Paul. "The answer, thank God, is that Jesus Christ can and does. He acted to set things right in this life of contradictions where I want to serve God with all my heart and mind, but am pulled by the influence of sin to do something totally different" (Romans 7:25 MSG).

Learning to Fight

This battle should neither intimidate us nor discourage us, because while our capacity to sin is as real as our need for God, it makes us dependent upon God's Spirit and His Word. If we are going to fight this spiritual battle effectively, then we need to feed our spiritual hearts spiritual food. Just as we feed our physical bodies nourishing food to keep them healthy, we battle spiritually by feeding our spiritual hearts spiritual food. When we allow God's Word and His Spirit to fuel our spiritual hearts, we come to grips with our own humanity and our deep need for God's help. This requires humility, and a man with a humble heart knows His need for God's Spirit to empower and energize him on a daily basis.

Unfortunately, the fleshly heart will never vanish until we die or until Christ returns. This side of death, we will always battle against our flesh. The reality of lust, arrogance, greed, selfishness, jealousy, unforgiveness, hatred, and envy will continue to tempt us, surprise us, and prod us. We go to battle by living in the light with our Father in heaven and with a few safe comrades who understand this war.

Ideally, if you're married, your wife is one of your safe friends. When my daughter first told us about her pregnancy, my wife, Joyce, and I did not tell another person for five days. We were too hurt and ashamed to tell anyone else. The enemy wanted to keep us isolated and turn our hurt into bitterness. I think of all of the people who no longer have a relationship with their children because they allowed the enemy to sour their hearts. They refused God's help and were too ashamed to share their needs with others.

I'm thankful that Joyce and I later shared our ordeal with others. In doing so, I was amazed at how many other people had faced the same pain with their daughters. In fact, two Promise Keepers speakers shared with me the fact that each of them had a daughter who became pregnant out of wedlock. I can't begin to tell you how they ministered to Joyce and me. The healing that began that day

> We go to battle by living in the light with our Father in heaven.

was so deep and so profound that, even as I write these words, my heart is thankful . . . and healed.

In my journey, I've learned that I battle for my heart by daily surrendering and yielding to God's leading and control over each and every day. The last thing I do when I leave my home for the office is to take my wife in my arms and pray over her and our youngest daughter, who is still at home. I pray that God gives us wisdom to know right from wrong and courage to do the right thing. I pray that God fulfills His purpose within the lives of my wife, our daughters, their husbands, and our grandchildren.

Experiencing the Victory

In the battle over my heart toward my daughter's pregnancy, the victory was fully realized in the delivery room. I had been summoned to the hospital. When I arrived, Joyce informed me that Erica, my daughter, was asking for her daddy. I entered the room and she said, "Dad, I'd like you to be in here. You can sit over here by the head of the bed."

While I had been in the delivery room for two of my own daughters' births, this was different because my girls were cesarean births. Erica's delivery would be a natural birth. As Erica's labor intensified, the nurse gave her new husband and Joyce instructions to support Erica's legs and to coach her breathing. After about ten minutes, Erica said to her tired mom, "Mom, why don't you let Dad do it?"

My heart pounded, and with wide eyes I looked at Joyce and asked if she thought it was okay. Joyce simply said, "Get over here before she starts her next contraction."

So there I was—holding one of my daughter's legs while my new son-in-law held the other. Within thirty minutes, the most incredible, miraculous, and wonderful event took place: I witnessed the birth of my third grandson, Isaiah. At that moment, all the hurt, all the pain, and all the disappointment vanished. The battle for my heart was won once again.

phase 1: awareness

My Heart

What makes your adrenaline flow? What lights up your heart? What kinds of stories, characters, and heroes cause your emotions to rise—even to bring tears to your eyes? What would you regret not doing or becoming if you were to die today? What would you do if you knew you could not fail? These kinds of questions tap into your heart for life.[2]

The purpose of the next awakening tool is to gain clarity about what God has written on your heart. Note where you are in the Awakening Experience Process—"My Heart" in Phase 1.

The Awakening Experience Process

Phase 1 **AWARENESS** *Awakening to Who I Am*	Phase 2 **FOCUS** *Awakening to God's Adventure for Me*	Phase 3 **PREPARATION** *Awakening to How I Must Live*	Phase 4 **FREEDOM** *Living the Awakened Life*
My Life in Christ **Taking Inventory** ***My Heart*** My Life Story My Giftedness	My Life Purpose My Life Vision My Life Mission The Primary Obstacles in My Path	My Guiding Convictions Personal Battle Plan Family Battle Plan Work Battle Plan Church Battle Plan Community Battle Plan	Friendship Battle Plan Guides Along the Way Time Analysis Life Journey Reviews
Where Am I Now?	Where Does God Want to Take Me?	How Must I Live to Get There?	How Will I Stay the Course?

Discovering what God has written on our hearts is one the most difficult things for men, in general, to discover and clarify. Wounds, sin, years of status-quo living, boredom, living other people's dreams for our lives, fears of failure, and myriad other things can silence and put layer upon layer over our hearts.

The following tool is designed to assist you, with God's help and insight from your friends, in peeling off these layers to discover the core of your heart. Follow these guidelines that explain the column headings on the heart discovery tool:

• **Heart probes:** Consider the categories and questions in the left-hand column, and reflect and write the specifics in the next column. Because story is a primary language of the human heart, many of the probes focus on stories, movies, or other artistic outlets that rouse your heart to life. These probes are designed to help you identify what you prefer and enjoy from different angles of interest. What Bible stories stir the most emotion in you? What Bible characters do you relate to the most? What movies and characters are your all-time favorites? What are your favorite sports, art, leaders, and heroes? Other probes ask you to identify the specifics about your dreams as a kid, your hopes for the future, what you would do if you knew you wouldn't fail, and identifying who you love and who loves you.

• **Themes:** When you look at what stirs your heart and why, what themes emerge? Do you see any similar traits or patterns in your answers? Perhaps you discover a heart for the underdog, the disadvantaged, or the poor. Or maybe you see a theme for tackling large and seemingly impossible odds. Or perhaps you discover a heart for the marketplace or becoming more involved in something specific. Some of the themes may be more general; others may be specific. That's okay.

• **My heart:** Now write one sentence or phrase that captures the essence of the themes you identified. For example, you might discover a heart to teach inner-city youth through sports and after-school activities. You might discover a heart to bring your faith into your company through your influence. You might discover a desire to mentor men in their twenties or to leverage your financial resources toward helping families be healthy. Take time with this statement. It should stir an energy and excitement in you, because it is tapping into what God has written on your heart. It is getting to your core.

• **Heart obstacles:** When Harold shared his heart response to his daughter's pregnancy, he battled anger, disappointment, and the fears associated with other people's perceptions and judgment. He also addressed the different sin-obstacles that the enemy incites to silence what God has written on our hearts. What are the obstacles that keep you from following and living what God has stirred you to be and do? Oftentimes, the fear of failure and the fear of financial uncertainty keep a man from moving forward. Or destructive and self-sabotaging habits severely limit or neutralize him. Many of us carry heart wounds that our parents or others inflicted on us at a young age. What about you? Identify the obstacles that you must acknowledge and address in this awakening process.

A completed heart analysis is also provided to illustrate how this tool works.

What are the obstacles that keep you from following and living what God has stirred you to be and do?

Awakening to What God Has Written on My Heart

Heart Probes	Specifics	Themes	My Heart	The Primary Obstacles to Living What God Has Written on My Heart
My Favorite Bible Stories and Characters				1.
My Favorite Movies and Characters				2.
My Favorite Sports and/or Art				3.
My Favorite Authors/Writers				
My Favorite Leaders				

Awakening to What God Has Written on My Heart

Heart Probes	Specifics	Themes	My Heart	The Primary Obstacles to Living What God Has Written on My Heart
My All-Time Heroes				4.
What I Would Do if I Knew I Wouldn't Fail				
What I Dreamed to Be and Do as a Kid				5.
What I Hope to Be and Do in My Future				
What I'll Regret if I Don't Do in My Lifetime				
Who I Love and Who Loves Me				

my heart ➤ Fictional Example
Awakening to What God Has Written on My Heart

Heart Probes	Specifics	Themes	My Heart	The Primary Obstacles to Living What God Has Written on My Heart
My Favorite Bible Stories and Characters	• David: his confrontation of Goliath and courageous leadership • Peter: his passion and risk-taking • Jesus in the Garden of Gethsemane	• A "freedom of the heart" theme	My heart is to experience and live free in Christ and to spread this message through life-on-life relationships that I have though my business opportunities. I long to do this in third world countries.	**1.** The fear of failure and the fear of what others will think if I follow my heart. **2.** I am susceptible to sexual temptation and need to stay honest and open with a few close friends and Lauren.
My Favorite Movies and Characters	• *Braveheart*: William Wallace and "Freedom!" • *Lord of the Rings*: Sam Wise Gamgee • *It's a Wonderful Life*			
My Favorite Sports and/or Art	• Soccer: the teamwork and competition • Football: the energy and pace • Monet: colors and setting	• The need for challenge and adventure in my life		
My Favorite Authors/ Writers	• Eldredge: how he stirs my heart • Grisham: how he weaves faith into fiction • Coelho: *The Alchemist* and life journey	• The desire to help other entrepreneurs to optimize their potential and to love and serve God		
My Favorite Leaders	• Winston Churchill: Never, never give up! • Abraham Lincoln: equality of all • George W. Bush: his conviction and freedom theme			

Heart Probes	Specifics	Themes	My Heart	The Primary Obstacles to Living What God Has Written on My Heart
My All-Time Heroes	• My dad: his perseverance and faithfulness • Jesus: gave up His will for the Father's • William Wallace: gave the commoners a vision for freedom			
What I Would Do if I Knew I Wouldn't Fail	• Create an international company that would train third world entrepreneurs to start businesses			
What I Dreamed to Be and Do As a Kid	• To play professional football • To find the love of my life, travel the world, and have a large family			
What I Hope to Be and Do in My Future	• To have a close, loving family with many grandchildren, to pour my life into younger entrepreneurs and share my faith with them	• To give my love and life freely to my kids and wife		**3.** The fear of financial loss and the pull of greed can keep me from taking risks for God's kingdom.
What I'll Regret if I Don't Do in My Lifetime	• Pour my all into my kids • Grow in depth and love with Lauren • To live what God has put on my heart • Help other people in need			
Who I Love and Who Loves Me	• Lauren • My kids • My family and a few close friends			

checkup

Time for a checkup. How is the process going for you? Are you and your friends encouraging each other? Are you stirring each other up to stay real, to go deep, and to cover each other with confidentiality, forgiveness, and grace?

Remember, you are still in Phase 1 of the Awakening Experience Process. You have driven a figurative stake in the ground with your letter to God. You have taken an honest assessment of all the different spheres of your life. And you have recently gained clarity on what God has written on your heart.

Are you becoming more aware of where you are *now* in life? Perspective is gained when we see things from various angles. That is what you are doing—seeing your life from different angles. The compilation of all these discoveries will give you honest, comprehensive awareness of where you are so that you can see where God wants to take you and how He wants you to get there.

Next, Buddy Owens is going to stir your heart and thinking in regard to hearing from God. The subject of God's speaking and our hearing Him is controversial and ambiguous to many—even in the church. Buddy's teaching on this subject is practical and real and easy to follow. After all, how can we gain clear awareness of who we are if God doesn't reveal it to us? And how can we know what God thinks about our life and future if we can't hear Him?

Stay engaged in the Awakening Experience Process. Stir each other up to stay encouraged and to advance through the awakening process.

Onward!

hearing from God

Buddy Owens

Speak, LORD, for your servant is listening.   —1 Samuel 3:9

Has God ever spoken to you? Would you recognize His voice if He did?

Hearing from God is not optional. It is absolutely necessary for the Christian life. Think about it for a moment. You are in a war for your life and your family. You have an enemy who hates you, and he never takes a day off. The whole purpose of the enemy's attacks is to separate you from God, and he will do whatever it takes to keep you from hearing from God—and from talking to Him.

A regular connection with the Lord is essential to your spiritual health. Hearing from God should not be a once-in-a-lifetime experience. Nor should it be an every-now-and-then experience. Hearing from God should be a daily experience. And He wants to hear from you every day too. As Carl Henry said, "Remember who your ruler is. Don't forget your daily briefing."[3]

Does God Still Speak Today?

Let me be the first to say that I have never heard the audible voice of God. But I know beyond any doubt or uncertainty that He has spoken to me countless times—bringing hope, comfort, encouragement, guidance, and conviction. Oftentimes His speaking is not so much in words as it is in certainties—a quickening in my spirit, a nudging in my conscience, a tugging on my heart, an out-of-the-blue remembrance of a seed of Scripture planted in my soul years ago and only just now coming to fruition at just the right moment—like turning on a light in a darkened room, and suddenly everything becomes clear.

The whole notion of God speaking can stir up controversy. Some people say God no longer speaks. But think how sad it must be for them to worship a God who won't talk to them.

To believe God no longer speaks is an unreasonable proposition. Does it make any sense that the God who created you, the God who gave His very own Son to die for you, the God who is so intimate that He actually dwells inside you by His own Spirit would now have nothing to say to you?

To believe God no longer speaks is a frightening proposition. Throughout Scripture, when God is present, He is speaking. If God no longer speaks, is He no longer present?

To believe God no longer speaks is a hopeless proposition. If God no longer speaks, then what makes us think He is listening?

God still speaks.

He speaks to us through the Scriptures; through the wise counsel of brothers and sisters in Christ; through providence bestowed or withheld; through circumstances, opportunities, and closed doors; and through the still, small voice of His Spirit speaking to our consciences, bringing conviction, comfort, or correction. A. W. Tozer wrote, "God is forever seeking to speak Himself out to His creation. He is, by His nature, continuously articulate. He fills the world with His speaking voice."[4] But *always* God's speaking is consistent with the Holy Scriptures. God will never violate His own written Word.

What Have You Been Trying to Hear?

Some people say, "Well, God has never spoken to me." I must ask them, "What have you been trying to hear? For whose benefit have you been listening?"

I believe hearing *from* God begins with the desire to hear *for* God. You might want to read that sentence again.

Far too often, we come to God with specific expectations. We

> He is always speaking. We just need to learn how to listen.

want to hear about a particular subject. We want to control the conversation. So we search the Scriptures looking for just the right verse to justify our preconceived position. Or we seek the counsel of one person after another until we finally hear what we want to hear. But that is not the way of a servant.

A servant listens to his master for the master's benefit, not his own. He receives instruction, correction, and encouragement for the furthering of his master's will. He hears from his master out of a desire to hear for his master. He hears what the master wants to say, and not simply what the servant wants to hear.

The servant's only question is, "What message does my Lord have for his servant?" (Joshua 5:14). The servant's prayer is, "Not as I will, but as you will" (Matthew 26:39).

We do not worship a silent God. He is always speaking. We just need to learn how to listen.

How Can You Learn to Listen to God?

With all the riot and racket of the world around you, how is it possible to hear that still, small voice and discover God's will for your life? The most important thing to remember is this: you get to know God's voice by getting to know His Word.

Let me give you three tips that might help you become a better listener:

1. First minutes. I practice what I call the habit of "first minutes." It's a habit of talking to God during the first minute of various activities throughout the day: the first minute after I get out of bed, the first minute in the shower, the first minute in the car on the way to work, the first minute in my office, and so on.

During these first minutes, I offer brief prayers of thanksgiving or ask for God's blessing. For instance, in the first minutes of the early morning I dedicate myself and my day to God, and I invite Him to fill me afresh with His Spirit. I ask Him to lead me and to use me for His purposes for that day. In my first minute in the car, I ask for God's protection and begin to pray for people or specific situations that come to mind. In my first minute at my office, I whisper a short prayer asking God to bless the work of my hands. On my way to a meeting, I ask God for wisdom and favor, and sometimes for courage to do the right thing.

Short prayers, simple thoughts with a heart turned toward God—these are prayers of surrender, asking for God's will to be done in my life.

These first-minute prayers keep my heart in a posture of surrender to God, and they help keep my ears attuned to God's voice. Oftentimes He will bring to mind someone or something I need to pray for. So I will pray right then and there. That doesn't mean I pull the car over and drop to my knees on the roadway. I just begin to talk to God about the situation as I'm driving or walking . . . for about a minute, sometimes longer.

2. Second thoughts. After walking with the Lord for more than forty years, if there's one thing I've learned it is this: God's direction rarely comes in monumental, cataclysmic revelations. It usually comes in minor course corrections, some of them almost imperceptible. In fact, I have found in my own life that I usually don't discover God's will until after the fact, when I stop and look back to see how He has faithfully guided my steps and led me to the right place in the right time.

Proverbs 3:6 says, "Seek his will in all you do, and he will direct your paths" (NLT). So having sought God's will in my first minutes, I now take Him at His word. By faith, I look to Him to direct my paths. Oftentimes, God's direction comes in the form of second thoughts. I might have second thoughts about a decision I have made or a course of action I am taking. It's not that I second-guess myself about everything, but the Holy Spirit will prick my conscience if I am starting to head down the wrong path. He might convict me of a sin or bring to mind someone I need to make something right with.

At other times, these "second thoughts" come, not as correction, but as confirmation in my heart that I am going in the right direction, and I find a refreshing awareness of God's presence and blessing.

3. Third dimensions. You learned back in your eighth grade geometry class that the first and second dimensions are the dimensions of distance—how far you can go in one direction or another. But the third dimension is the dimension of depth. Now you're probably wondering what that has to do with hearing from God. Well, I'll tell you: the third dimension is the most important dimension when it comes to daily devotions. And the best piece of advice I can give you about reading your Bible is this: read for depth, not for distance.

Let me give you a word picture of what I mean. Reading your Bible for distance is like skipping a stone across the surface of the American River behind Sutter's Mill. (Just to jog your memory, that's where the California Gold Rush started.) It's fun to impress ourselves or our friends with how far we can skip the stone. We like to see how fast we can throw it and how many times we can make the stone bounce across the water's surface. That's what reading for distance is: we want to see how far and how fast we can skip across the surface of the Scripture: "I read three chapters today in five minutes!"

But reading for depth is like stopping at one spot on the riverbank and looking down into the water. As you look beneath the surface, you begin to see how clear and how deep the water is. Then you start to see life teeming in its depths. And then you spot a little gold nugget gleaming in the riverbed. The longer you look, the more nuggets you find; and the more nuggets you find, the richer you become. That's what it's like to read for depth. You don't want to see how far and how fast you can skim over the surface; you want to see how deep you can go and how much wealth you can mine from just one verse or phrase or passage.

You have now entered the third dimension of devotions. It's in these times and in these depths that you will most often and most clearly hear the voice of God calling you to a deeper level of trust, beckoning you to greater acts of faith, whispering sweet words of affirmation and hope, and sometimes shouting truths that will rock your world. This is where hearing begins . . . in the depths of the Scriptures where untold riches await you.

What Do You Do with What You Have Heard?

What next? What do you do with what you have heard? I believe that's a question God asks all of us. So often I catch myself waiting or wanting to hear from God, and then I hear His gentle reminder: *What have you done with what I've already told you?* I'm waiting for God to tell me something new, but all the while He is waiting for me to act on what I already know. After all, why should He waste His time giving me new instructions if I haven't been obedient to His previous instructions?

Just as important as what you hear is what you do with what you hear. Just as hearing from God is not optional, neither is obedience. If you don't like what God says to you, you can't put your fingers in your ears and pretend you didn't hear Him. You're not fooling anyone—especially not God. But when you act on what you know, then you will know more.

If you want to hear from God, start each day with an open heart, open hands, open ears, and an open Bible. Let your prayer be, "Speak, Lord, for Your servant is listening."[5]

Just as hearing from God is not optional, neither is obedience.

THE AWAKENING EXPERIENCE PROCESS

phase 1: awareness

Learning to Hear God's Voice

If we awaken to God's voice, as Buddy has compelled and helped us to do, then the adventure of life takes on an entirely different flavor. In fact, you could complete the awakening process—even develop an incredible life map with intriguing battle plans—but if you don't hear God's voice in the process, then you have a man-made life map. But if God's perspective—His thoughts, feelings, and desires for your life—is infused into your discoveries, then you have a God-inspired life map! And that's what you want.

The following tool is designed for you to capture and log what you are hearing in your life journey. As you engage your first moments, second thoughts, and third dimensions with God in prayer, what are you hearing from God as you reflect upon what you discovered in the taking inventory tool? What are you hearing from God as you gain clarity on your heart and what He has written on it?

Just as expedition captains logged their discoveries on dangerous adventures, so we need to log our discoveries with God in living the awakened life. Use the following tool to do so. Use these guidelines for this tool:

• **What I'm hearing:** Write what you believe God is communicating to you in the different categories of your life: your personal life, home life, work life, church life, community life, and friendships. Use this format, or one like it, to add new entries. As you journey through life with God, He wants to lead you. As He leads you, you will hear from Him. You want to record what He tells you.

• **Supporting sources:** Identify any supporting biblical or other sources that give you an anchor or reference point to what you are hearing. As Buddy said, God will never tell you something that is in direct violation or contradiction to His written Word. What verse or passage of Scripture provides the foundation for what you are hearing? Additionally, perhaps your friends or others have validated what you have heard. Or your pastor may have preached on the same thing right after you heard from the Lord. Add your supporting sources to what you are hearing.

• **What I must do:** Buddy asked the question, "What do you do with what you have heard?" Add these points of action in this column. You will refer to these when you develop your battle plans in Phase 3 of the Awakening Experience Process.

As with the other awakening tools in the process, a fictional example is provided to illustrate how you can use this tool. Remember that you can download all of the awakening tools at **www.promisekeepers.org/AwakeningExperience**, keep them in your computer's hard drive, and customize them as you wish. You will want more copies of this "Hearing from God" log as life unfolds.

"What do you do with what you have heard?"

what i'm hearing from God
Summary of What He Is Telling Me

Life Category	What I'm Hearing	Supporting Sources	What I Must Do
Personal Life			
Home Life			
Work Life			
Church Life			
Community Life			
Friendships			

Life Category	What I'm Hearing	Supporting Sources	What I Must Do
Personal Life	I need to learn how to fight the enemy's temptations against me—specifically in the area of sexual temptation.	Ephesians 6:10–18 1 Thessalonians 4:3–5 Pastor John's recent sermon	I need to open up to my small group. Ask them to help me with Internet temptation.
	I need to start taking care of my physical body. I am not in control of my appetite and physical health.	1 Corinthians 6:19	I need to ask Lauren to help me put together a plan.
Home Life	I need to forgive my dad for leaving our family as kids and not being there at critical times in my life.	Matthew 6:14–15	Write a letter to my dad in my journal, even though he has died.
	I am not alert to the enemy's tactics to infiltrate my home. I need to secure these things spiritually.	Ephesians 6:10–18	I need to talk to Jerry about how to pray spiritually about this.
	Lauren is God's gift to me. I am not pursuing her heart like I want to.	Ephesians 5:25–31	I will ask for her forgiveness and plan weekly date nights with her.

what i'm hearing from God ►Fictional Example
Summary of What He Is Telling Me

Life Category	What I'm Hearing	Supporting Sources	What I Must Do
Work Life	God is asking me to leverage my business relationships and opportunities to pour my life and talents into third world entrepreneurs.	1 Timothy 6:18 My lunch with Sam last week	I will call my contact in India and tell him what I'm thinking.
Church Life	I'm not using my real gifts and talents at church. God wants me to explore starting a ministry to help third world entrepreneurs.	1 Corinthians 12:4ff	I will meet with Pastor John, share my heart, and go from there.
Community Life	Mrs. Zambers needs help in our neighborhood. She is a widow who needs home repairs done.	1 Timothy 5:3	I will rally Tom and Sere to help me fix her porch stairs and insulate her attic.
Friendships	God is asking me to open my heart to its deepest caverns with Jake and Manny.	Proverbs 17:9; Galatians 5:1, 13	I will let them into my struggles with temptation and my heart to help third world entrepreneurs.

checkup

It's checkup time. Are you still in the process? Are you and your buddies advancing, stirring each other up? Learning to hear God's voice may be a new process for you. Remember, living the awakened life is a journey, and the tools designed in the awakening process are not do-it-once-and-move-on exercises. Rather, they are designed to equip you to stay the course and live the life God made for you.

To this point, you have written your letter to God, taken inventory, and gained clarity on what He has written on your heart. You now have insight and a tool to log what you are hearing from God. You are adding to your ability to have clear perspective of the different aspects of your life. Remember, the Awareness Phase is about seeing your life from different angles.

You will now go deeper in discovering who you are. Reggie Dabbs will stir your thinking and heart with his life story and insights. You will map out your life on a life graph, capture the critical insights from it, and discover your unique giftedness.

Stay encouraged. Stir each other up. Keep each other on the path and adventure of the awakening.

Onward!

Learning to hear God's voice may be a new process for you.

discovering your unique design

Reggie Dabbs

I am a high school motivational speaker. I speak in schools all around the world. About nine months ago, something happened at a school on an island called Tasmania, off the coast of Australia. It took three days for it to hit me.

The first day I was there, I was watching the kids enter the auditorium. Most came in laughing and giggling, like all high school kids do. But about the time we were ready to start the program, I saw a young man walking toward the door. He was the perfect island boy. He had blond hair and blue eyes. I watched him walk toward the door that was closed and run right into it. It caught me off guard, and I kind of laughed. But as the boy stumbled back, he swung his right arm around, revealing a red and white cane—the symbol that tells the world he is blind. I quickly stopped laughing as I watched the teacher take him by the arm and help him find his seat. I thought about him briefly afterward.

The next day I was in another school. A teacher stood beside me during the entire program, using sign language to communicate to kids who could not hear me. I tried to locate the kids who were deaf, but I never did find them. I thought it was a boy on the third row, in the middle, until he put his arm around a girl and said, "Hey baby, how ya doin'?" I figured that he wasn't deaf!

On the very next day, the third day in a row, I was in still another school. The principal said, "Wait just one more second. There are some more kids coming in. Let's wait for them to get here." The side door to the auditorium opened, and I watched nine boys in wheelchairs roll down a ramp. I watched and admired them.

Every kid I just described to you is limited or crippled in some way. The thought that occurred to me on the third day was simply this: *everybody is crippled.*

I am absolutely humbled to write in a book like this one—written by great authors, great preachers, great men of God. I consider myself the least of all the men who contributed to this book. I think it's because of my past. I'm starting to figure out why Promise Keepers asked me to write a chapter called "Discovering Your Unique Design." I think it's because I know my past and how it has crippled me in life. And knowing this has helped me discover what God thinks about me.

You see, I believe everybody is crippled. All of us have something in our lives that is trying to drag us down. As I watched the blind kid walk into the door and the teacher sign to deaf students and the nine boys in wheelchairs roll down the ramp, I was overwhelmed with how much I adore kids like these. Why? Because they are doing something that I hope, wish, and pray I would be able to do if I were in their position. If I were in a wheelchair, I'd want to roll my chair where everybody else walked. If I were blind, I'd want to sit where everyone else could see. If I were deaf, I'd want to hear with my eyes what everyone else can hear with their ears. But as I said, I believe everybody is crippled.

> All of us have something in our lives that is trying to drag us down.

My Story

For me, it's a simple story. Many of you have heard it at a Promise Keepers conference. I grew up in foster care. My mom started having children at a very young age. She had a son and twin girls. She was trying to feed her babies, so she asked a man for help. He said if she would sleep with him, he'd give her twenty dollars for food. She did. I am the result of that twenty-dollar bill.

My mom had a schoolteacher who told her students, "If you ever need help, call me." So my mom called the teacher. This teacher found my mom and her kids and took them to her home. That schoolteacher and her husband, the school janitor, taught and took care of my mom until the day I was born.

The day I was born, my mom screamed in the delivery room, "I don't want it! I just don't want it!"

The teacher asked, "What do you want me to do?"

She said, "You take it."

So I was raised by my mom's favorite schoolteacher and the school janitor. They taught me about the love of Jesus. They taught me the Word of God.

I remember my second grade parent-teacher conference. For me, parent-teacher conferences meant that my parents met with the teacher, then I got in trouble when I got home. But on this particular night, I noticed something a little strange. Everybody else's mom and dad were young. My mom and dad were old. On the way home, I asked, "Mom, Dad, why are you so old?" Now that question can invite a good whipping in a lot of families in America, but my parents understood. That night was the first night I heard my whole story.

When my parents told me my story, they said things like, "You can't change your past, but you can change your future. Reggie, Jesus knows everything about you. He made you for a purpose." I liked these words. I also liked it when my foster mother called me her "Little Moses."

Your Story

What's your story? What makes you crippled? What is in your past that is trying to pull you down and keep you from becoming what God made you for? What is it in your life that makes you sit up at night and watch TV, flipping through the channels instead of going to sleep like everyone else? What is it in your life that keeps you awake in bed even when you're tired? Maybe you are one of those people who have to put on your headphones or listen to the radio instead of falling asleep like everyone else.

Have you ever been without a TV, radio, or music, and you begin thinking about your past and get really depressed? Do you ever tell yourself, "If I knew then what I know now, I never would have done that"? Or, "If I knew then what I know now, I never would have gone there"? Then the conversation in your head says those two words that really hurt: "Why me?" If you've ever said these kinds of things to yourself, then you're probably like me.

Do you know what God thinks about you and me? I do, because the key scripture for this chapter tells me. It's Psalm 139:14–16. Listen to what these words say about us:

> I praise you because I am fearfully and wonderfully made; your works are wonderful, I know that full well. My frame was not hidden from you when I was made in the secret place. When I was woven together in the depths of the earth, your eyes saw my unformed body. All the days ordained for me were written in your book before one of them came to be.

I learn a lot about what God thinks about me in these verses. What I learn in these words has set me free from my crippled past and helped me see how uniquely God made me. It's changed the way I think, the way I live, and the way I relate to other people. I believe it can do the same for you.

Think Differently

You have to start believing what God thinks of you. You have to stop looking at your life, your story, with your own eyes. You must start looking at your story through the eyes of Jesus Christ. In my own eyes, I'm nothing but a twenty-dollar bill. But in the eyes of Jesus, I'm perfect. Psalm 139:14 says, "I praise you because I am fearfully and wonderfully made; your works are wonderful, I know that full well."

How can the son of a prostitute, whose mom gave him away, really believe what God thinks about him? Because I started to realize that the very first thing I *must* do is think differently about

You must start looking at your story through the eyes of Jesus Christ.

myself. I need a whole new mind-set about who I am, why I was created, and why I am here on earth. So do you!

If you used to do drugs, you don't do drugs anymore because Jesus has set you free. If you were from a broken home, you're not from a broken home anymore because Jesus has set you free and made you a part of His family. If you feel like life has slapped you around and you're thinking about suicide, you don't have to go there anymore because Jesus has set you free.

But the next step after being set free is to begin to think differently about *who you are*.

You may need to write on a three-by-five-inch index card: "Think differently." And then do it! Tape the card on the bathroom mirror or on the rearview mirror in your car. Put it in places where you will see it every day so that when you get up and do your normal routine, you will start thinking differently about yourself. Because, guess what? Jesus Christ made you. He "fearfully and wonderfully" made you. That's why you can praise Him—because you are "fearfully and wonderfully made." So the first thing you must do is think differently!

Let me give you an example. When David faced Goliath, everyone saw a giant, but David saw an opportunity. When David went to the giant, everyone thought he would die. But David knew he would win. Scripture even says that David *ran* to face Goliath. Why did he run? Because he was thinking differently. He knew who he was in God's eyes.

Live Differently

The second thing you must do is live differently. Live your life the way God intended you to live it. You have to understand that Jesus Christ did not create you to live a crippled life. He made you to live a life running—running for Him! The main scripture for Promise Keepers in 2004 was Psalm 119:32: "I run in the path of your commands, for you have set my heart free." You see, that's vital. The foundation to this whole thing called life, before we do anything else, is to know that Jesus Christ has set us free. He set us free from our crippling past, with all its pain, hurt, and sorrow. He set us free so that we can run in the path of His commands. So begin to live differently.

The blind man in Mark 10:46–52 is an example of how to do this.

Then they came to Jericho. As Jesus and his disciples, together with a large crowd, were leaving the city, a blind man, Bartimaeus (that is, the son of Timaeus), was sitting by the roadside begging. When he heard that it was Jesus of Nazareth, he began to shout, "Jesus, Son of David, have mercy on me!"

Many rebuked him and told him to be quiet, but he shouted all the more, "Son of David, have mercy on me!"

Jesus stopped and said, "Call him."

So they called to the blind man, "Cheer up! On your feet! He's calling you." Throwing his cloak aside, he jumped to his feet and came to Jesus.

"What do you want me to do for you?" Jesus asked him.

The blind man said, "Rabbi, I want to see."

"Go," said Jesus, "your faith has healed you." Immediately he received his sight and followed Jesus along the road.

What happened in this story? A blind man named Bartimaeus sat on the side of the road. He heard Jesus was coming. He longed for something to happen in his life. He knew Jesus Christ could do that. So he began to cry out, "Jesus, Son of David, have mercy on me!" The crowd tried to stop him, but he wouldn't stop. In fact, Scripture says, "He shouted all the more, 'Jesus, Son of David, have mercy on me!'" Sometimes you can't listen to the crowd—to what others are telling you to do. You can't listen to the people who know your past, who know your story and try to keep you from becoming what God wants you to be. God is able to change the hardest of hearts. He changed mine, and He can change yours too!

Blind Bartimaeus began to scream, "Jesus, Son of David, have mercy on me!" Finally, Jesus stopped and said, "Bring him to me." It's ironic that the very people who told him to be quiet, who tried to shut him up, then brought him to Jesus. What you have to see in this story is this: when we call out to Jesus, no matter what our story is, no matter how blind we are, Jesus will hear us. He will stop, He will call you, and He will touch you!

There is one small but significant detail in this story. It is what blind Bartimaeus did before he went to see Jesus. You see, you have to remember that Bartimaeus was still blind in verse 49! The verse reads, "Jesus stopped and said, 'Call him.' So they called to the blind man, 'Cheer up! On your feet! He's calling you.'" The point I don't want you to miss is in verse 50: "Throwing his cloak aside, he jumped to his feet and came to Jesus." You see, back in that time if you were blind, crippled, or lame and showed you had some type of deformity, they would give you a special jacket to wear so everyone would know you were blind or crippled. The cloak that Bartimaeus wore that day gave him the right to sit on the side of the road and beg for money. That cloak represented blind Bartimaeus's story.

Before he could see—before Jesus healed him—Bartimaeus stood up, took off his cloak, and threw it aside. Before he could see, he threw aside his past and cast his life before Jesus Christ—the good, the bad, and the ugly. He gave everything about himself to Jesus. You could say he began to live differently even before Jesus changed him!

Now let's take a look at Jacob. You may have heard the story of Jacob in the Old Testament and how he wrestled with the angel all night. The angel touched his hip, and Jacob lived the rest of his life with a limp. You see, it's plain and simple. I'd rather go through my entire life with a limp given to me by God than to live my whole life being normal without God. Sometimes our story, our past, makes us limp. But it is awesome to know that he whom the Son sets free is "free indeed" (John 8:36). Jesus Christ has set us free.

So we must think differently, live differently, and lastly, we have to relate differently.

Relate Differently

The last verse in our key scripture, Psalm 139:16, says, "All the days ordained for me were written in your book before one of them came to be." God knows every day of every person who has ever lived. Did you know that? He knew us when we were still forming physically and not even born. And He knows all our days on earth since we were born. Think about this. Do you realize how unique you are? Do you realize how unique I am? Even with all our flaws and the pain from our past that cripples us, God made each of us amazingly unique.

The Bible is filled with people who are absolutely unique. Some people think that God loves the men and women in the Word of God more than He loves us. I don't believe that. I think He makes every one of us unique and loves us all the same.

Take David. When he faced Goliath as a young man, he couldn't wear the armor of Saul. It didn't fit. Besides, it wasn't him. He had to go with what he knew, with what he had. He was so unique that God used a slingshot in David's hand—something David knew how to swing and throw—to conquer the giants of the land. Consider Gideon. He was absolutely petrified of battle. But his love for God was so huge that he went anyway. And God used him, flaws and all. Moses didn't like to speak because he stuttered so badly. But his passion for God was so large and his love for his people was so strong, he faced Pharaoh and proclaimed, "Let my people go." Joseph's family threw him in a hole and sold him for money as a slave.

Despite all the terrible things that happened to him—despised by his brothers, thrown into jail for twelve years for something he didn't do, forgotten for two years by a friend from jail who was released before him—he never got bitter. Instead, Joseph later saved his own family, who had disowned him and left him to die. You see, each and every life story is unique—in Scripture and in life today. I could go on and on. Ruth, Esther, Mary, Zechariah, and Jonah. There are so

> You see, each and every life story is unique—in Scripture and in life today.

many stories of unique people in the Book that God put together.

I remember as a boy going to Vacation Bible School. They taught us that God put the Bible together as a map for us. If we would only read about the people in the Bible, their stories could help us through the things that we go through in everyday life. What I found out about all these people in the Bible is that they are all different, yet all the same. They are all unique, yet made in the image of God. And I completely believe that the scripture is true: "All the days ordained for me were written in your book before one of them came to be." God made us all unique.

God knew my pain. He knew my hurt. That's why Jesus went to the cross. That's why He died for me. And that's why He died for you. We are unique. Because we are unique, we can relate to each other uniquely. You see, when you look at what Jesus Christ has done in your life, when you've given Him your life—your story with its crippled past—you begin to think and live differently. And when you understand how God uniquely made you, then you begin to relate to the world in a completely new way. You begin to relate differently.

Incredible Plans

Psalm 139:15 says, "My frame was not hidden from you when I was made in the secret place. When I was woven together in the depths of the earth." Here's what I take away from this verse. One day God the Father, God the Son, and God the Holy Spirit were making something. A lot of the angels came around to check it out. As they were watching, one angel asked, "God, what are you making?"

God said, "I'm making a little boy."

One of the angels said, "He's kind of a chubby little guy, isn't he?"

God laughed and said, "I'm going to call him Reggie."

The angels said, "Oh, that's a cool name. Is this Reggie special?"

God said, "They are all special. I make each and every one of them with My own hands. They are all unique. Each person has a special place for Me."

One of the angels said, "What will this Reggie do?"

"Well, to start, he'll have a lot of hurt. He'll have a lot of pain. But in the end, I have an incredible plan. If you want, you can read it in the book." (Remember Psalm 139:16: "All the days ordained for me were written in your book.")

The angels went over to the book, and they began to read. "Wow, he's going to work with Promise Keepers. That's awesome!"

God says, "Yes, he will work with Promise Keepers. He will also have a wife and a son, and he's going to do wonderful things for Me."

Can you put yourself in that story today? Can you see Jesus making you and discussing how unique you would be? Can you see that despite the hurt and pain that He saw when He made you, in the end He saw how your uniqueness would make you incredibly useful to Him?

In Matthew 28:18–20, Jesus Christ tells us right before He ascended into heaven:

> All authority in heaven and on earth has been given to me. Therefore go and make disciples of all nations, baptizing them in the name of the Father and of the Son and of the Holy Spirit, and teaching them to obey everything I have commanded you. And surely I am with you always, to the very end of the age.

You see, when we follow Christ, we have to relate differently to the world. The world is full of hopelessness and pain, hurt and sorrow. But one person who has been touched by God can do so much.

Realize Uniqueness

We must begin to realize who we are in Him and who God has created us to be. He created us to be His unique child with a unique story to be told for those without hope in the world. It's important that you understand that Jesus Christ knows your story. He knows your past. If we give Him everything in our lives, then He is able to

We can give peace where there is no peace. We can give love when there is no love.

touch us in a way that changes how we think, how we live, and how we relate to the world. And then we can give hope where there is no hope. We can give peace where there is no peace. We can give love when there is no love. And people in the world are waiting for someone to love them.

So who are you? Not in your own eyes, but in the eyes of Jesus Christ. Once you find that out, you begin to think differently, live differently, and relate differently.

"Reggie," you ask, "how do I do that? How do I find myself in Him?"

You must realize that nothing in your past is unforgivable. Here's a promise you can count on: "If we confess our sins, he is faithful and just and will forgive us . . . from all unrighteousness" (1 John 1:9). More than that, the Bible tells us that Jesus came to set the captive free. Galatians 5:1 says, "Christ has set us free to live a free life" (MSG). So if you have given your life to Jesus, you are free from your past and free to be who He uniquely created you to be.

You've already read about the battle of a man's soul. You've already read about the battle of a man's heart. You've already read about hearing the voice of God. Now you are learning in this chapter what you can do with your uniqueness. You can think differently because you are a child of the King. You can live differently because He has a purpose for you. And you can relate differently to your family, church, and community as someone who has been set free by Jesus Christ.

Who are you . . . in God?

THE AWAKENING EXPERIENCE PROCESS
phase 1: awareness

My Life Story

Reggie just told us that each of us has a story to tell. And you learned at Promise Keepers that your story is part of a larger story: the epic, cosmic battle between God and Satan. Your life story has been and will be an adventure filled with unanticipated and unpredictable twists and turns. Your life journey has had its ups and downs, its mountaintop experiences and dark valley seasons.

In this next exercise, you will be guided through a process to develop a life graph of your significant high and low points. Then you will glean the critical lessons from your life journey so far. This insight into your life experiences is a vital component of awakening to who you are and to God's unique vision and purpose for your life.

Remember, we are progressing through a process, the Awakening Experience Process.

The Awakening Experience Process

Phase 1 **AWARENESS** *Awakening to Who I Am*	Phase 2 **FOCUS** *Awakening to God's Adventure for Me*	Phase 3 **PREPARATION** *Awakening to How I Must Live*	Phase 4 **FREEDOM** *Living the Awakened Life*
My Life in Christ	My Life Purpose	My Guiding Convictions	Friendship Battle Plan
Taking Inventory	My Life Vision	Personal Battle Plan	Guides Along the Way
My Heart		Family Battle Plan	
My Life Story	My Life Mission	Work Battle Plan	Time Analysis
My Giftedness	The Primary Obstacles in My Path	Church Battle Plan	Life Journey Reviews
		Community Battle Plan	
Where Am I Now?	Where Does God Want to Take Me?	How Must I Live to Get There?	How Will I Stay the Course?

As you can see on the chart above, we are still in Phase 1: "Awareness." You have given your life to Christ. You have taken inventory of your life and discovered your primary issues right now, you have gained insight into what God has written on your heart, and now you are going to gain insight into your life journey, or life story.

The writer of Hebrews refers to followers of Christ as "strangers and exiles on the earth" (11:13 NASB). We are passers-through. We are destined to something unbroken and unscathed by sin—eternity with God in His kingdom.

We do not know the number of days God gives us on earth. But Reggie just gave us insight into what God thinks about our life from Psalm 139:14–16. We learned that God knows us from the day we were conceived in our mother's womb and that He comprehends how many days and years we will live physically on earth. David even implies that the content of those days are not a mystery to God. Reflect on these words again:

> For You formed my inward parts; You wove me in my mother's womb. I will give thanks to You, for I am fearfully and wonderfully made; wonderful are Your works, and my soul knows it very well. My frame was not hidden from You, when I was made in secret, and skillfully wrought in the depths of the earth; Your eyes have seen my unformed substance; and in Your book were all written the days that were ordained for me, when as yet there was not one of them. (Psalm 139:13–16 NASB)

As Reggie said, not one day, week, month, or year of your life—past, present, or future—is a mystery to God. That is hard to grasp! How often do memories in our past feel more like senseless, disconnected, and haphazard events?

This next step in the Awakening Experience Process is to gain clarity and insight into your story. To do so, you will map out your life journey on a life graph. Your life graph will give you a snapshot of all the life-altering experiences you have had to date.

What is a life-altering experience? A life-altering experience is something in your life that left its imprint on you and has in part shaped who you are today. These experiences can be negative or positive. Reggie discovered he was the result of twenty-dollar bill—a potentially life-paralyzing discovery in and of itself. But Christ rescued him and helped him discover what God thought of him—the most revolutionary life-changing event of his journey. These are two very profound life-altering events.

Reggie ended his chapter with the question: "Who are you . . . in God?" To answer that question, you will start by listing all of your life-altering events. Together, these events, experiences, and people have significantly shaped who you are today. Your life altering events include:

What events
have changed
who you are
and where you
are in life?

- **Spiritual reference points:** When the Holy Spirit convicts a person of his sin and need for God and that person responds with a confession of sin and profession of newfound faith in Jesus Christ, that is a life-altering experience. He will never be the same. At other times in our lives, we drift away from God and choose to return to Him. Some call these moments in time rededications. What spiritual experiences have you had with God that have changed who you are today?

- **Relationships:** Oftentimes, God brings into our life at a critical juncture a person who changes our life. Camp counselors, coaches, parents, teachers, friends, and mentors can all leave their imprint on us and affect who we are today. Are there people in your history who have altered the course of your life, to the extent that you would not be who you are or where you are in life without their influence?

- **Season-of-life events:** Graduation from college, marriage, the birth of a child, becoming a grandparent, the death of a parent, and other profound season-of-life events can also alter the course of your life. What events have changed who you are and where you are in life?

- **Life-changing experiences:** Positive and negative experiences can alter the course of our lives. Positive events may include overcoming the odds in an athletic sport or other interest, gaining acceptance into an institution or new job, helping another person succeed, a summer at camp, or other positive experiences that have helped shape who you are today. Negative events may include personal illness, bankruptcy, divorce, adultery, addiction, or getting caught doing something illegal. What life experiences—events, scenarios, encounters—have left an indelible mark on your life and have partly shaped who you are today (how you think, live, and relate)?

On the following page, list the life-altering events in your life. In this process, you want to capture *all* of the events that have altered the course of your life journey in one way or another (positively or negatively). The reason is that you will later discover connections, patterns, and themes as you see your life story laid out in your life graph.

Be careful not to add to your list profound memories that didn't necessarily change your life. You want to identify all the events, experiences, and people who have altered your life in some way, but be careful to not create them out of highlights or lifetime memories (things that you will never forget but that didn't really affect the course of your life).

For each life-altering event, identify your age at the time, what specifically happened, whether it was a high point or low point in your life, and the outcome. A completed, and fictional, life-altering list illustrates how to use this tool.

People, Experiences, and Events That Have Changed My Life

My Age	Summary	High Point / Low Point?	Outcome

life-altering events
People, Experiences, and Events That Have Changed My Life

My Age	Summary	High Point/ Low Point?	Outcome

People, Experiences, and Events That Have Changed My Life

My Age	Summary	High Point/ Low Point?	Outcome
8	I gave my life to Christ at Mountain View Community Church.	High	I forged a lifelong relationship with George B., who invited me to church.
10	My parents divorced.	Low	I was torn between Mom and Dad. Dad abandoned us.
12	I confronted a neighborhood bully.	High	I learned to confront opposition in a positive way.
15	The desire to compete is awakened in me.	High	Coach Stife helped me see my potential in football and incited the desire in me to excel.
17	I got my girlfriend pregnant, and she had an abortion.	Low	The unthinkable happened. I was devastated and still carry the pain of what I did today. Dad was absent.
19	I rededicated my life to Christ.	High	I realized how far I drifted from God. Drew S. led me back to God at S.U. my freshman year.
24	I married Lauren.	High	She is God's gift to me. I would not be who I am today without her.

life-altering events ▶ Fictional Example
People, Experiences, and Events That Have Changed My Life

My Age	Summary	High Point / Low Point?	Outcome
26	I was fired from my first job.	Low	I questioned my abilities and purpose in life.
29	I was mentored by Rich H.	High	God sent him to guide and mentor me and help me discover what it means to be a godly husband and worker.
31	Our first baby, Caleb, was born.	High	There is nothing like seeing your own flesh and blood born. I will never forget this experience. Our family expanded.
34	Dad died of lung cancer.	Low	We never connected like I long to connect with my kids. He died angry and lonely. I wish we could have reconciled our past.
38	I launched my new business.	High	I have learned that I have more potential than I thought. I love the freedom, creativity, and leadership opportunities.
41	My current life juncture	?	I am at a crossroads. I want to be more of a spiritual leader to Lauren and my kids. I am not content to just work to make money. How can I connect to God's kingdom more actively? What does God want me to do?

Now that you have identified all of your life-altering experiences, plot them on the following high-point/low-point life graph to the degree that they were high and low. Again, a fictional completed life graph plots the example life-altering points. Use the middle row to plot your age span and the bottom row to identify the life chapter themes of the different seasons of your life journey. For example, one might have a life chapter entitled "Foundations Laid" or "The Dark Years" or "Sowing My Wild Oats Years" or "Return to God Years."

Look at life breaks in your life graph and then do your best to summarize each life chapter. You may need the help of friends or your wife to help you identify life-chapter breaks and how to title each one.

Identify the life chapter themes of the different seasons of your life journey.

my life graph
The Highs and Lows of My Life Story

High Points	Age	Low Points	Life Chapters

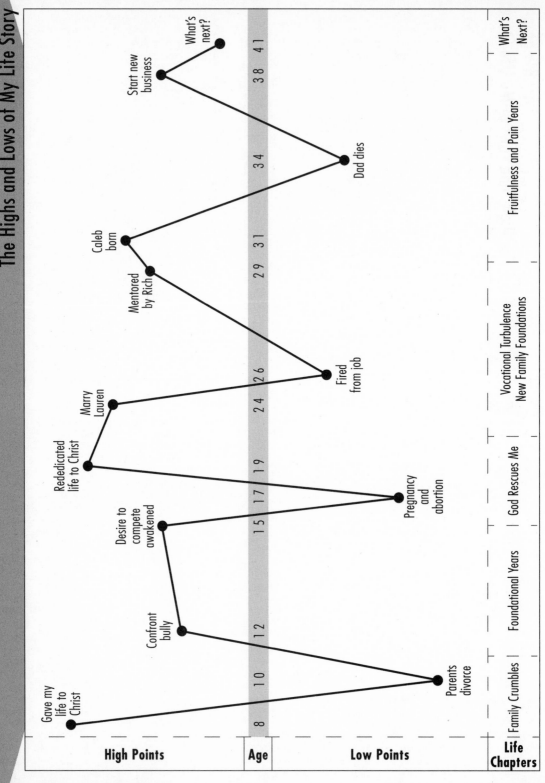

my life graph ▶ Fictional Example
The Highs and Lows of My Life Story

High Points
- Gave my life to Christ
- Desire to compete awakened
- Rededicated life to Christ
- Marry Lauren
- Mentored by Rich
- Caleb born
- Start new business
- What's next?

Age
8 10 12 15 17 19 24 26 29 31 34 38 41

Low Points
- Parents divorce
- Confront bully
- Pregnancy and abortion
- Fired from job
- Dad dies

Life Chapters
- Family Crumbles
- Foundational Years
- God Rescues Me
- Vocational Turbulence / New Family Foundations
- Fruitfulness and Pain Years
- What's Next?

To view our lives on a life graph helps us connect experiences that otherwise feel random and haphazard. When we see the continuity and themes of our life journey, we begin to understand God's faithfulness in new and fresh ways. We see that He has been present in the highs and lows of our life stories, and He has rescued us even in dark, painful seasons of life. We come to terms with controlling forces, other than God, that have restricted us for entire chapters of our life—forces like an absent dad, the pursuit of money and position, sexual sin, or a drive to prove ourselves to others. We may also discover that God used an experience or person in our youth to plant seeds in our lives that later took root and produced significant fruit (e.g., a leadership talent awakened playing sports, an artistic interest sown by a patient teacher, a desire for third world missions awakened on a trip to Latin America, and so on).

As Reggie wrote in his chapter, when we bring the good, bad, and ugly to God and see our stories from his perspective, we think, live, and relate free of the controlling forces of our past. We're also free to follow Christ wherever He might lead us, in a way that is true to our life purpose and His vision for us. But first we must gain His perspective on our journey. We must be awakened to God's thoughts and understanding of our life stories.

Now that you have mapped out your life graph, it's vital that you capture the critical learning points from it. Spend time studying and reflecting on your life graph. Use the following questions to help you capture themes, patterns, and the critical takeaways from this Awakening Experience Process tool. Again, a fictional example is provided.

Awakening to What God Wants Me to Learn About My Life Story

Questions	Insights
Governing Factors What forces have governed the direction of my life at various stages?	• • •
Key Connections Are there any significant connections between events in my life story?	• • •
Patterns What patterns emerge in my life journey?	• • •

life journey insights
Awakening to What God Wants Me to Learn About My Life Story

Questions	Insights
God's Faithfulness Where do I see God's faithful hand guiding my life?	• • •
Implications Do I learn anything about who God wants me to be and what He wants me to do in my future?	• • •
Other Discoveries Do I learn anything else from seeing my life-altering events with all the high and low points?	• • •

Awakening to What God Wants Me to Learn About My Life Story

Questions	Insights
Governing Factors What forces have governed the direction of my life at various stages?	• My dad's abandonment of our family left a void in my heart at a young age. Though I never reconciled with him before his death, I now see how God wants me to forgive him and allow Him to fill that void in my heart. • Where was Dad when I encountered the bully and was going through the tough years as a 17-year-old?
Key Connections Are there any significant connections between events in my life story?	• God sent Rich into my life at a critical time to be a spiritual dad to me and to help me understand God's desires for me as a follower of Christ, husband, and dad. • Coach Stife was also a godsend at a critical time in my life and helped me to transfer my competitive drive to positive outlets in business.
Patterns What patterns emerge in my life journey?	• I have always been a leader and survivor. • I am not afraid of risks. • I have learned that God brings fruitfulness and wholeness out of pain and brokenness.

life journey insights ►Fictional Example
Awakening to What God Wants Me to Learn About My Life Story

Questions	Insights
God's Faithfulness Where do I see God's faithful hand guiding my life?	• God helped me through the pregnancy and abortion as a teenager. I know He has forgiven me and that I will meet my unborn child in heaven someday. • Coach Stife and Rich were gifts from God to me. • Where would I be without Lauren? I want to learn how to love her more and grow in our relationship.
Implications Do I learn anything about who God wants me to be and what He wants me to do in my future?	• I do not want to repeat the mistakes of my dad in my own family. I feel that any problems and issues in my marriage and family can be worked out. It is not worth running, like my dad did. • I am a natural leader and entrepreneur. When I feel boxed up in a situation, I get bored and need change or I lose heart.
Other Discoveries Do I learn anything else from seeing my life-altering events with all the high and low points?	• Do I learn anything else from seeing my life-altering events with all the high and low points? • I am at a "What's next?" juncture. My heart wants to live my life not for myself but for God and His kingdom. I am open to going and doing whatever He wants me to do. • I'm eager to discover God's purpose and vision for my life.

phase 1: awareness

My Giftedness

How are you doing in this awakening process? Are you gaining clarity on your life? Remember, you are still in Phase 1. The goal in this phase of the process is to awaken to the man God created you to be. You began by writing a letter to Him, thanking Him for the gift of forgiveness of sin, eternal intimacy with Him, and freedom from darkness and the enemy of your soul. Then you discovered what God has written on your heart. You may still be processing your heart. As you learn to hear God's voice, as Buddy Owens taught you, clarity will grow. With the preceding awakening tools, you focused on your life story and have begun to see your life from God's vantage point.

Do you see how awareness or perspective evolves? We ask the right questions, dig deeply and honestly, listen for God's voice, and begin to experience breakthrough. Confusion dissipates. We come to terms with our uniqueness. We stop trying to be someone we are not, and we flourish in living the life God created us to live.

But remember, this is a process. Don't rush the process. If you are stuck or restless with your discoveries so far, then use your small group to probe and help you move toward clarity. Or bring your wife into your discoveries, if you are married. You may want to meet with your pastor and gain his insights into your discoveries. But bottom line: hear from God. Get away from the noise of life and hear His whispers (or thunder!). Continue to invite Him into your thinking and reflection. He will guide you.

The next and last exercise to help you awaken to who you are is a tool designed to help you gain clarity on what God has invested in you—to discover your giftedness. You can see the Awakening Experience Process map in Phase 1:

> "All kinds of things are handed out by the Spirit, and to all kinds of people!"

The Awakening Experience Process

Phase 1 **AWARENESS** *Awakening to Who I Am*	Phase 2 **FOCUS** *Awakening to God's Adventure for Me*	Phase 3 **PREPARATION** *Awakening to How I Must Live*	Phase 4 **FREEDOM** *Living the Awakened Life*
My Life in Christ **Taking Inventory** **My Heart** **My Life Story** ***My Giftedness***	My Life Purpose My Life Vision My Life Mission The Primary Obstacles in My Path	My Guiding Convictions Personal Battle Plan Family Battle Plan Work Battle Plan Church Battle Plan Community Battle Plan	Friendship Battle Plan Guides Along the Way Time Analysis Life Journey Reviews
Where Am I Now?	Where Does God Want to Take Me?	How Must I Live to Get There?	How Will I Stay the Course?

You have God-given gifts. He gave some of them to you when you were born. Some people call these gifts natural talents or abilities. In athletics, we say that a kid has God-given speed or jumping ability or arm strength. In music, we say that a person has a God-given ability to listen to music and then play what he hears. Or we say that someone is a natural leader or natural actor. When we apply discipline, repetition, and practice to our natural abilities, then we become a master, expert, or professional in that area of skill. We all have natural talent, and God is the giver of all of it.

God also gives those in Christ spiritual gifts when they are spiritually born again. Paul says in 1 Corinthians 12:4 that "God's various gifts are handed out everywhere; but they all originate in God's Spirit" (MSG). He doesn't forget anyone. "Each person is given something to do that shows who God is: Everyone gets in on it, everyone benefits. All kinds of things are handed out by the Spirit, and to all kinds of people! The variety is wonderful: wise counsel, clear understanding, simple trust, healing the sick, miraculous acts, proclamation, distinguishing between spirits, tongues, interpretation of tongues. All these gifts have a common origin, but are handed out one by one by the one Spirit of God. He decides who gets what, and when" (1 Corinthians 12:7–11 MSG).

Your natural talents and your spiritual gifts come from God. They are His gifts to you. If you are going to live a spiritually awakened and alert life in Christ, then you must gain clarity on what gifts He has given you. The following tool will guide you through a process to do so with a series of questions in the left-hand column.[6]

• **What do you love to do?** We all love to spend our time and energy doing certain things. What do you love to do so much that when you do it, time speeds up? You can burn hours doing things you love and not realize it. What ignites the passion deep in your gut and propels you into motion? For example, some love to build things, fix things, and learn how things work. Others love the world of thoughts and ideas. They love to read and debate and think about something from all different angles. Others love to compete in sports or the arts. They are passionately driven to surpass their personal best. What do you love to do?

• **If you could do anything for a living, what would you do?** This question is similar to one of the heart-probe questions you contemplated in chapter 2: what would you do if you knew you would not fail? Remove the fear of failure and finances and ask yourself that question. What occupation would you choose? What activity would bring you the most joy? What activity would allow you to master the gifts God has given you? Would you make a living working with your hands? Or with your head? Or with both? Would you lead an organization? Or would you be a secondary leader or not a leader at all? Would you help people? If so, how would you help them? Ask yourself these kinds of questions to get to the core of your answer.

• **What are you really good at?** Step back from yourself (figuratively) and observe what you are good at. Some are good at details. Others are good at analyzing or synthesizing data. Some are good at thinking of new ways to do things. Some are good at fixing motors

> What ignites the passion deep in your gut and propels you into motion?

or building houses or cracking the code on a mysterious illness. Some are good at presenting a compelling case before a judge. Others are good at researching and writing. Some are great with people and can sell almost anything. Some are great with people and can reconcile almost any kind of conflict. Some manage people or processes very well. Some are strategic visionaries and think very systematically. What are you good at?

• **What have others told you that you're really good at?** This question may help you discover a gift that you otherwise wouldn't see. For example, you may not feel that you have an inquisitive, sharp mind; but other people consistently tell you that they are amazed at how you think. Or other people may have told you that you listen very well or that you have an ability to teach complex concepts in a clear and understandable way. What have others told you over the years that you are good at?

• **What fascinates you?** Perhaps you have an insatiable desire to learn about history or cooking or the NFL football draft prospects. What is it about what fascinates you that pulls you toward it? What intrigues you about it? And what do you do when you are pulled into the realm of what fascinates you? Try to get into the activity of what fascinates you and discover that natural abilities are set into motion when you are in that zone.

• **Where does your thinking drift when it is free to do so?** This question comes at your giftedness from a slightly different angle than the previous question. When the weight and pressure of your world are not heavy on your mind, what do you think about? Do you think about restoring, rebuilding, or inventing things? Do you think about helping people? If so, how do you imagine yourself helping them? Do you think about ministering to people in some way? If so, what are you doing? And where are you doing it? Oftentimes, we gravitate in our thinking toward zones of activity and contemplation roused by God's giftedness in us. Where does your thinking drift when it is free to do so?

• **What do you miss doing that you are no longer doing?** Your answers to this question offer another glimpse into your God-given giftedness. Many feel trapped in their current situation—and outside their zone of giftedness—feeling that they could never go back and still pay their bills. Or the responsibilities of family or promotions at work or involvement at church pulls us away from what we used to love to do—and were very good at. What do you miss doing that you are no longer doing?

• **What are you proud of that you have done in your lifetime?** Take a minute and brag about yourself. Your answers may not be typical résumé statements. You might be proud of the deck you built or the class you taught to young married couples or the brochure you created for your company. Think about what you are really proud of—things you've done or the type of person you have become—and write your answers.

After you have reflected deeply and honestly in response to these questions, look for themes in your answers. Write the themes or similar answers in the column to the right. And then summarize these themes in the "My Core Giftedness" column. These core gifts and talents represent what God has invested in you. Ultimately, He wants you to optimize these gifts and use them for His glory and for His purposes on earth.

As with the other Phase 1 tools, a fictional example of a completed giftedness profile is provided to help you see how this process works.

These core gifts and talents represent that which God has invested in you.

my giftedness
Awakening to What God Has Invested in Me

Key Questions	Details	Themes	My Core Giftedness
What do I love to do?	• • • •	•	
If I could do anything for a living, what would I do?	• • • •	•	**1.**
What am I really good at?	• • • •	•	**2.**
What have others told me I'm really good at?	• • • •		

Key Questions	Details	Themes	My Core Giftedness
What fascinates me?	• • • •	•	
Where does my thinking drift when it is free to do so?	• • • •	•	3.
What do I miss doing that I'm not doing?	• • • •	•	4.
What am I proud of that I've done in my lifetime?	• • • •		

my giftedness ►Fictional Example
Awakening to What God Has Invested in Me

Key Questions	Details	Themes	My Core Giftedness
What do I love to do?	• Learn about history and contemplate the nature of God. • Create return on value in business investments and invest in God's kingdom. • Design and build homes and developments.		
If I could do anything for a living, what would I do?	• Invest all that I've learned about business into helping young, third world entrepreneurs grow in skill and ability.	• I am good at strategy and identifying new opportunities.	**1. Entrepreneurial Leader:** I have the ability to find new investment opportunities with high-yield return on investments.
What am I really good at?	• Finding good investments with a good return rate. • Negotiating deals. • Building trust and team.	• I am an effective team leader.	**2. Communicator:** I have a gift to teach complex concepts in clear, compelling deliveries.
What have others told me I'm really good at?	• That I work well with people. • That I'm a savvy businessman. • That I'm a clear communicator. • That I'm a good, strategic thinker.	• I am a clear communicator.	

Awakening to What God Has Invested in Me

Key Questions	Details	Themes	My Core Giftedness
What fascinates me?	• The world economy and market. • Best business practices. • Cutting-edge leadership methods with solid ethics. • The world of ideas.	• I have a gift to find strong return on investments.	
Where does my thinking drift when it is free to do so?	• To exploring new real estate opportunities. • To how I could teach others in less fortunate places in the world what I've learned and encourage them to go for it. • To strategies on how we could bring the gospel to others in more effective and efficient ways.		**3. Primary Leader:** I am gifted to lead teams and have the experience to do so.
What do I miss doing that I'm not doing?	• Building wood furniture in my wood shop. • Deep sea fishing. • Leading teams on work projects. • Teaching others about God, His love for them, and how they can know Him.	• I am good fixing things with my hands and figuring out how to do so.	**4. Builder:** I have the skill to build and fix things and can do so by leading a project or doing it myself.
What am I proud of that I've done in my lifetime?	• Helped our church save thousands of dollars on its building project. • Leading the building crew on the missions trip in Brazil. • Helping 85-year-old Mrs. Abers get her furnace fixed. • Teaching next-level leadership to the international sister company when I worked in my last job.		

checkup

Congratulations! You have ventured through Phase 1 of the Awakening Experience Process. Are you encouraged? Have you gained clarity on who you are . . . in God? Do you need to return to some of the awakening tools and update them with new thinking?

Remember, these tools are designed for you to customize, keep fresh with new discoveries (with edits and updates), and to lead you toward clarity. That is why it is best to download the awakening tools at **www.promisekeepers.org/AwakeningExperience**, keep them in your computer, change them, add to them, and update them regularly so that they help you move toward living the life God created you to live.

The tools in Phase 1 progressively build on each other as the arrow in our Awakening Experience Process map illustrates:

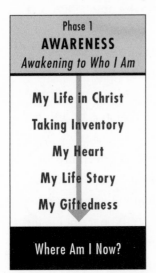

| Phase 1 |
| **AWARENESS** |
| *Awakening to Who I Am* |
| My Life in Christ |
| Taking Inventory |
| My Heart |
| My Life Story |
| My Giftedness |
| Where Am I Now? |

You learned something about yourself with each tool. You expressed gratitude, confession, and trust in Christ with your letter to your heavenly Father. You took an in-depth assessment of your life with the inventory tool. You gained insight into what God has written on your heart for life. You graphed your life story and discovered God's faithfulness and how He has prepared you uniquely in light of your journey. And you have clarity on your giftedness—the core spiritual gifts and natural talents that God has invested in you.

Go back through your findings in each of these tools. You may want to break out of your world for a few hours, a half day, or even a full day and reflect on your discoveries so far. Ask God what He thinks. Are you on track? Do you have any blind spots? Allow His Spirit to stir your spirit. Allow yourself to hear His thoughts and feelings toward you.

And keep each other encouraged, stirred up, and pursuing God's mind and heart in this process. Refrain from trying to fix a buddy if he is stuck. Be creative in how you can rouse one another's desire to tap into God's heart and perspective. This is a *process*—a spiritual process. And we need each other to help us stay engaged and to advance toward living the unique life God has designed for each of us.

We will now move into Phase 2 in the Awakening Experience Process—awakening to God's adventure. Bishop Joseph Garlington will rouse your heart and passion for life. Hang on as you read his chapter. His slant on life purpose, vision, and mission is refreshing and inspiring.

Life is an adventure, and you want to live God's adventure for you. But you have to tap into His purpose, vision, and mission for you if you are going to live that adventure. All of the perspective you've gained in Phase 1 has prepared you to craft your unique life purpose, life vision, and life mission statements. The awakening tools after Bishop Garlington's chapter will guide you through a process to do so.

Onward!

►embracing your life vision, purpose, and mission

Bishop Joseph L. Garlington, PhD

There are a few words in the human language that I call "really big" words. These words are transcendent—eternal in their scope, encompassing unspoken desires and dreams, and summarily dismissing the trivial and the mundane. Really big words rise above common language and cultural barriers. They attract attention without really drawing attention to themselves. Like really big people, when really big words appear, they have the capacity to demand our interest without a sense of intrusion. These words are electric and create sparks, especially when they touch that eternal deposit that God places in every created person. They unleash deep stirrings that we are helpless to suppress.

In recent years, one really big word in particular has resurfaced in the collective consciousness of incredibly diverse people—it's everywhere you turn. This word is *purpose*.

Ironically, nowhere is this word seizing the attention in conversations in venues all over the world more than in the work of an amazing Christian minister whose best-selling book, *The Purpose Driven Life,* has been on the *New York Times* bestseller list for months. In a recent interview with Bill O'Reilly on the Fox Network's news program *The O'Reilly Factor*, Rick Warren said that he is receiving thousands of letters from non-Christians who are deeply interested in the thesis of the book. Pastor Rick says that the most important question you can ask in life is, "What is my purpose?"

Four hundred years ago, Blaise Pascal, a brilliant seventeenth-century scientist and a committed Christian, said, "There is a

God-shaped vacuum in the heart of every man which cannot be filled by any created thing, but only by God the Creator, made known through Jesus Christ."

But thousands of years before Pascal was born, the writer of Ecclesiastes said of the Creator:

> He has made everything beautiful in its time. He also has planted eternity in men's hearts and minds [a divinely implanted sense of a purpose working through the ages which nothing under the sun but God alone can satisfy], yet so that men cannot find out what God has done from the beginning to the end. (Ecclesiastes 3:11 AMP)

"A divinely implanted sense of purpose." Think about this phrase for just a moment and then ask yourself, "What is my divinely implanted sense of purpose?"

If you Google the term *God gene*, you will find articles and books dealing with the question: "Is faith 'hardwired' into the very fabric of our lives?" When God created us, did He "plant" the reality of Himself in each one of us? Pascal seems to say, in effect, that the only thing that can fill the "God-shaped vacuum" must be the "God-shaped God." I like to say that there are no atheists, because God didn't create anything that doesn't believe in Him.

Imagine that you're out for a walk in the woods or on the beach and you suddenly come upon a totally unfamiliar object. In that brief moment, your mind would formulate an elementary question: "What is this?" An amplified version of that question, however, would more than likely be, "For what purpose is this thing in existence?" Or maybe we would say, "I wonder what somebody had in mind when they made this thing?" And if we were just a little more curious, we would begin to seek out someone who could tell us what the object is and what its purpose is.

I would like for us to examine four biblically fundamental concepts concerning who we are. These four and some others

I like to say that there are no atheists, because God didn't create anything that doesn't believe in Him.

are included in a dialogue the Lord God had with the emerging prophet Jeremiah. It is the inauguration of an awesome ministry that God is about to entrust to Jeremiah, and he is struggling:

> Now the word of the Lord came to me saying, "Before I formed you in the womb I knew you, and before you were born I consecrated you; I have appointed you a prophet to the nations." Then I said, "Alas, Lord God! Behold, I do not know how to speak, because I am a youth." But the Lord said to me, "Do not say, 'I am a youth,' because everywhere I send you, you shall go, and all that I command you, you shall speak. Do not be afraid of them, for I am with you to deliver you," declares the Lord. Then the Lord stretched out His hand and touched my mouth, and the Lord said to me, "Behold, I have put My words in your mouth. See, I have appointed you this day over the nations and over the kingdoms, to pluck up and to break down, to destroy and to overthrow, to build and to plant." (Jeremiah 1:4–10 NASB)

Jeremiah needed to embrace four essential pieces of information that the Lord God gave to him. Let me paraphrase each of them:

- "Before I formed you in the womb I knew you" (v. 5).
  ▶ *Your existence preceded your conception.*

- "Before you were born I consecrated you" (v. 5).
  ▶ *Your purpose preceded your birth.*

- "Do not say, 'I am a youth'" (v. 7).
  ▶ *Your believing must precede your seeing.*

- "I have appointed you a prophet to the nations" (v. 5).
  ▶ *Your assignment preceded your awareness.*

Let's examine each one of these liberating insights that God gave to Jeremiah. Because all of these are universal principles, we can apply them in the life of every man.

Here is the situation. Jeremiah is actually trying to find some "wiggle room" in order to avoid this new task. Let's just call him a draft dodger. Jeremiah is seeking to convince the almighty God that he is totally unqualified for the task; and furthermore, he is informing God of the reasons he believes that he does not qualify.

Unwillingness is a normal response when God calls upon men to do something. A very elementary study of the Scriptures will reveal that most of the Lord's servants reacted the same way when summoned. This deep reluctance to believe in his worth or in God's preparation to serve Him must stem from either a sincere humility or a profound sense of inferiority. There seems to be an inherent question in each person's response to the Creator: "Who am *I* to do this thing?"

If there is any truth to the axiom "Heroes are not born; they're cornered," then God "cornered" Abraham, Moses, Gideon, King Saul, David, and Saul of Tarsus. Simply put: if God ever gets you cornered, just say, "Yes, Lord." All of these men did—eventually.

We Have a Purpose That Is Unassailable

No weapon that can hurt you has ever been forged.   —Isaiah 54:17 MSG

A familiar commandment accompanies the unveiling of one's purpose when serving God: "Do not be afraid of them, for I am with you to deliver you" (Jeremiah 1:8). And it is not very long into the serving that you discover *why* He commands you not to fear.

Because they had a vision of their future and an understanding of what they would have to do in order to get there, faithful men of the Bible were fully engaged with their life purpose. Obstacles became opportunities that eventually helped them to accomplish their goals.

Whenever someone like David connects with his purpose, he is more conscious of his destiny than of his death. He is more concerned for the harm to the sheep than the hunger of the bear or lion. He is more disturbed by Goliath's profanity than by Goliath's pride. He is absolutely convinced that "all things" are working together with all of those "other things" and that God's intention is to produce something that God calls "good."

No one created in God's image is illegitimate.

Let's consider the critical truths with which we must come to terms before embracing our life purpose. The first one is this: *your existence preceded your conception*. You were already someone who existed before the seed was "planted" in your mother's womb! You did not begin on earth; you started in heaven, in the very heart of God and in His eternal counsels. Paul told the Ephesians:

> Long ago, even before he made the world, God chose us to be his very own, through what Christ would do for us; he decided then to make us holy in his eyes, without a single fault—we who stand before him covered with his love. His unchanging plan has always been to adopt us into his own family by sending Jesus Christ to die for us. And he did this because he wanted to! (Ephesians 1:4–5 TLB)

"I knew you," God says. It is a sovereign affirmation. It is a divine declaration. It is irrefutable proof of your very existence. God is not playing divine word games with us; you really cannot *know* something unless it actually has existence. This is an incredible truth, especially in light of the feelings of many men who were born out of wedlock and were mislabeled as illegitimate. No one created in God's image is illegitimate. What is of major importance is not who you came *through*, but Who you came *from*.

The second critical truth is this: *your purpose preceded your birth*. When Isaac's wife Rebecca became pregnant, she inquired of the Lord God concerning the turmoil that was taking place in her womb; and God gave her some critical information concerning the life purpose of the twins. This God-given information enabled her to oversee the son with the promise (see Genesis 25:22–23).

Compare her assignment with the truth expressed in *The Amplified Bible*, which says, "Train up a child in the way he should go [and in keeping with his individual gift or bent], and when he is old he will not depart from it" (Proverbs 22:6). The purpose God revealed to Rebecca became her priority for Jacob's life.

Where do we see *purpose* in God's words to Jeremiah? God wrapped it snugly in another word in the phrase translated "Before you were born, I *consecrated you*" (Jeremiah 1:5; emphasis added). This is the familiar Hebrew word *qadash*, which means sanctified, set apart, to be hallowed and dedicated to a specific purpose.

To illustrate, the day my wife saw me walking out of the kitchen on my way to the garage with one of her cherished ten-gallon stainless steel gourmet cooking pots, she asked a very simple question: "What are you going to do with my pot?" Her question, roughly translated, was a very serious inquiry concerning my intentions in removing the pot from its normal environs. A season of "intense fellowship" began precisely at the point of my informing her that I had planned to use it to wash my SUV. During this fellowship time, she thoroughly convinced me that the particular pot in question was essentially a "sanctified" pot. She did not use the word *consecrated*, but she made it abundantly clear that it was set apart for cooking food and *not* intended for washing trucks. I then proceeded to seek out something that was "less honorable" and deemed more suitable for my cleansing task. We never had that discussion again.

Purpose, very simply, is the reason for which something exists. There is a good reason for your existence: God created you to accomplish something for Him. A profound truth is that God created you to fill a need; and His intention is to utilize everything about you, including your height, size, color, gifts, talents, abilities, predispositions, temperament, preferences, intellect, and even the time and place in the plan of God when you live out your existence on earth. Absolutely everything about you is of His sovereign disposition.

The psalmist said, "Our lives are in his hands" (Psalm 66:9 NLT). The apostle Paul told the Athenians that God had "determined their appointed times and the boundaries of their habitation" (Acts 17:26 NASB).

As in the case of Jeremiah, it takes God to tell me why I am here. Any other purpose for my life, other than my created purpose, is no

> Absolutely everything about you is of His sovereign disposition.

different from my kitchen-pot illustration and is an offense to the One who created me. Any pursuit that ignores or dismisses God's original intention for your life will produce frustration and ultimately failure. A pastor of a very large church in Central America motivates each one of the many thousands in his congregation with this powerful insight: "I will never be satisfied until I am fulfilling my purpose."

In the movie *Chariots of Fire*, Eric Lidell's sister tried to demonstrate a conflict of interest in the life of the Scottish missionary as he sought to compete in the 1924 Olympics while preparing for the mission field. He lovingly responded with these words: "God made me for a purpose, and that purpose is China; but He also made me fast, and when I run, I feel His pleasure." Because Eric was fully in touch with his purpose, he had a heightened sense of God's presence in his life and a fuller understanding of Isaiah's declaration that "no weapon that can hurt you has ever been forged" (Isaiah 54:17 MSG). He could confront the pressures of conscience from the royal family of Great Britain and from his natural family. Eric demonstrates the power of purpose as a primary source of courage when he needed courage for two different arenas: the world and the church.

We Have a Vision That Is Attainable

A basic need of all human existence is a vision of the future in which one has enough faith to act. —*Futurist* magazine, 1977

Vision is an inspired look at reality. —Charles Simpson

I can see you in the future, and you look much better than you look right now. —A prophetic song

The third critical truth is this: *your believing must precede your seeing.* "Do not say, 'I am a youth'" (Jeremiah 1:7). God's revelation to Jeremiah concerning his life is shocking; and Jeremiah's famous "Alas, Lord God" could be paraphrased: "Lord God, if *I'm* all You have to use, You are in deep trouble." Jeremiah then begins to inform the Lord God of his own insights concerning some flaws that God must have overlooked.

First, he says, "I do not know how to speak" (Jeremiah 1:6). However, God had already heard this excuse from Moses. Jeremiah then tells the Lord about his age problem, but the Lord had already dealt with the other side of that argument from Abraham.

When the Lord commanded him, "Do not say, 'I am a youth,'" He was saying to Jeremiah, "Don't tell *Me* who you are, let Me tell *you* who you are!" Like Gideon, Jeremiah was having trouble seeing what God saw in him. *Credendo vides* is the Latin phrase that means "By believing, one sees." Jesus sharply reminded Martha, just before He raised Lazarus from the dead, "Did I not say to you that *if you believe, you will see* the glory of God?" (John 11:40 NASB; emphasis added). Jeremiah, Moses, Abraham, Gideon, Saul—all of them— they didn't have a *seeing* problem; they had a *saying* problem.

Most of us are familiar with the idea that confessing sin is agreeing with God concerning His viewpoint on our behavior. The Greek word *homologeo* means to say the same thing as another; and while this is important in the matter of God's perspective concerning sinful behavior, it is equally important in the matter of God's viewpoint concerning your purpose and His plan for your life. Do not try to tell God who you are; you really don't know who you are until He reveals it to you. When He tells you who you are, agree with Him whether you see it or not, because God is always right.

When Art Linkletter asked a little boy, "What do you want to be when you grow up?" the boy responded tersely, "Alive." Vision asks, "*Where* do you want to be when you grow up?" Vision is a living, vibrant picture of the future; it is compelling and convincing and when you are in touch with it, you have taken a major step of faith.

Paul told the Philippians, "I press on to take hold of that for which Christ Jesus took hold of me" (3:12). Believing what God says *to* me and what God says *about* me is prerequisite to seeing what God sees *in* me. When God's Word tells us who we are and what we are, we

> The only vision that is ever truly attainable is the one He planted in your heart.

must not dispute His word to us, even though we may be struggling with others' words concerning us. His words are truth.

The Lord gave Gideon a picture of the future—a vision of how He saw him—*before* He gave Gideon a mission. He called him a "valiant warrior" (Judges 6:12 NASB). God gave Abraham a picture of Abraham's future when he declared that He had already made him "the father of many nations" (Genesis 17:4). Romans 4:17 tells us that God "calls things that are not as though they were."

One of my mentors, Dr. Derek Prince, taught, "All progress in the Christian life is by faith." The writer of Hebrews says, "Without faith it is impossible to please God" (11:6). When God tells you who you are, He also orders you not to contradict His words with your words. In essence, He is saying to us, "Do not say the opposite of what I am saying to you; you can't *please* Me if you don't believe Me."

Many of us know people who are completely frustrated with their lives as they are struggling to produce a vision that is not their own. They are not living out the vision for their lives the Father had in mind, and they have become the ones described by Thoreau as, "The mass of men [who] lead lives of quiet desperation." The only vision that is ever truly attainable is the one He planted in your heart. Genuine vision can only be released by your expressed willingness to accept it by faith, no matter what it is.

We Have a Mission That Is Possible

It's not possible for a person to succeed—I'm talking about *eternal* success—without heaven's help.
—John 3:27 MSG

When God made me, He made me fast; and when I run, I feel His pleasure.
—Eric Lidell, in *Chariots of Fire*

The fourth critical truth is this: *your assignment preceded your awareness.* Webster's Collegiate Dictionary defines *mission* as "a specific task with which a person or a group is charged." If Jeremiah had been wrestling with the age-old question "Why am

I here?" then he is suddenly face to face with the one Person in the universe who can give him the answer: "I have appointed you a prophet to the nations." In other words, "You are here to speak for Me to My people."

Even though Jeremiah is reluctant to agree, I'm reasonably convinced that he wasn't surprised. How could he be? God had designed him to function as a prophet, and everything about his nature was in harmony with that design. Jeremiah's internal compass was pointing him in this direction all along. Like all of us, he had an intuitive sense about the rightness of God's words to him.

"I have appointed you a prophet to the nations" (Jeremiah 1:5). This is not the movies. The Lord God is not saying to him, "Your mission, if you choose to accept it . . ." Your mission is your assignment, and it is never optional; it is the key to your purpose and your vision. You can't ever be truly happy until you are engaged in the tasks that are accomplishing your particular mission.

Divine assignments are usually validated by several key principles that seem to accompany them.

- Assignments—all of them—will have enemies seeking to resist them. Billy Crystal once said, "If David didn't have Goliath, he would have been just another kid throwing rocks."
- Assignments will have both destructive and constructive aspects: "to pluck up and to break down, to destroy and to overthrow, to build and to plant" (Jeremiah 1:10 NASB).
- Assignments will always have opposition. Great opportunities will have equally great opposition: "For a wide door for effective services has opened to me, and there are many adversaries" (1 Corinthians 16:9 NASB)
- Assignments will require courage. Usually a God-given assignment will be accompanied by the admonition, "Do not be afraid."
- Assignments will have an inherent promise of God's presence. He says, "I will be with you" (Joshua 1:5).

> Your mission ...is never optional; it is the key to your purpose and your vision.

- Assignments will always require obedience. Paul told King Agrippa, "I did not prove disobedient to the heavenly vision" (Acts 26:19 NASB).

I'm often asked the question, "How can I know God's will for my life?" My answer is always the same, "Tell Him you'll do whatever He wants you to do." There is a principle for living that I have found in John 7:17: "If anyone is willing to do His will, he will know of the teaching, whether it is of God or whether I speak from Myself" (NASB). In essence, if you're willing to do God's will, He'll tell you what it is. You can't operate from a point of view of suspicion when you're walking with God. I've even heard some people say, "But if I tell Him I'll do whatever He wants, He could tell me anything!"

Here are some basic principles that have been helpful to me and to those I lead:

- Admit that you can't do whatever it is that God wants you to do without His grace (see John 15:5).
- Accept your helplessness in finding the will of God and know that it's His responsibility to get you there (see Job 11:7).
- Acknowledge your need to walk daily by the standards you know, and trust Him to reveal the ones you don't know (see Philippians 3:16–17).
- Accelerate your own process by celebrating the existence of your assignment: even if you don't know *what* it is, you do know *that* it is (see Hebrews 11:10).
- Apply the powerful principle of commitment when faced with hard choices. "Roll your works upon the Lord [commit and trust them wholly to Him; He will cause your thoughts to become agreeable to His will, and] so shall your plans be established *and* succeed" (Proverbs 16:3 AMP).

Twenty-five years ago, I had a transforming moment when I first heard the following quotation from W. H. Murray. Instantly, I knew why I had either succeeded or failed in various endeavors in my life.

This truth has become a guiding principle for me and for thousands of others: I need to commit.

Until One Is Committed

Until one is committed, there is hesitancy,
the chance to draw back, always ineffectiveness.
Concerning all acts of initiative (and creation), there is
one elementary truth, the ignorance of which kills
countless ideas and splendid plans: that the moment one
definitely commits oneself, Providence moves too.

All sorts of things occur to help one that would never otherwise have occurred. A whole stream of events issues from the decision, raising in one's favor all manner of unforeseen incidents and meetings and material assistance, which no man could have dreamt would have come his way.

I have learned a deep respect for one of Goethe's couplets:

Are you in earnest? Seize this very minute.
Whatever you can do, or dream you can, begin it.
Boldness has genius power and magic in it.
Only engage and then the mind grows heated,
Begin and then the work will be completed.[7]

The moment a man actually embraces the reality of his life purpose, vision, and mission, he lights the fuse to an explosion that will be heard all over the world. He comes to terms with the why of his existence and the where of his journey. He is about to discover the unlimited resources available to him in order to fulfill his mission. He will have obstacles to overcome, but like Henry Ford once said, "Obstacles are those frightful things you see when you take your eyes off your goal."

No one has yet figured out how to stop a man who is completely in touch with his purpose and with his destiny.

No one has yet figured out how to stop a man who is completely in touch with his purpose and with his destiny.

THE AWAKENING EXPERIENCE PROCESS

phase 2: focus

My Life Purpose, Vision, and Mission

What are you thinking and feeling after reading Bishop Garlington's chapter? Did he not reach into your heart and jolt it to life with his insight into God's perspective of our life purpose, vision, and mission? He, like the other gifted authors in this book, is operating in the zone of his purpose and mission. God has equipped and gifted him with the ability to discover and communicate insight, truth, and application to men.

The question for us is, how can we clarify and craft our own unique life purpose, vision, and mission statements so that we venture the path God wants to us travel?

The Awakening Experience Process

Phase 1 **AWARENESS** *Awakening to Who I Am*	Phase 2 **FOCUS** *Awakening to God's Adventure For Me*	Phase 3 **PREPARATION** *Awakening to How I Must Live*	Phase 4 **FREEDOM** *Living the Awakened Life*
My Life in Christ Taking Inventory My Heart My Life Story My Giftedness	*My Life Purpose* *My Life Vision* *My Life Mission* The Primary Obstacles in My Path	My Guiding Convictions Personal Battle Plan Family Battle Plan Work Battle Plan Church Battle Plan Community Battle Plan	Friendship Battle Plan Guides Along the Way Time Analysis Life Journey Reviews
Where Am I Now?	Where Does God Want to Take Me?	How Must I Live to Get There?	How Will I Stay the Course?

Before we begin to write these statements, let's reorient ourselves to our current location in the Awakening Experience Process. As you can see on the chart above, we have finished Phase 1. You have gained clarity and awareness about how God designed you. We are now moving into Phase 2, called "Focus—Awakening to God's Adventure for Me."

Once you are awakened to who you are, how then does He want you to live? For what unique purpose did He create you? Where does He envision you in the future of your life?

What mission must you accomplish in your lifetime so that you might fulfill "God's purpose in [your] own generation" (Acts 13:36)?

The following tool in the Awakening Experience Process is designed to guide you through a process to write your life purpose statement, life vision statement, and life mission statement. You will also identify the primary obstacles in your way of living the adventure God wants you to travel. In writing these statements, you will gain a focus that will help you strategically maneuver through the unknowns of the future. It's as if you will be looking at your life through a pair of binoculars and adjusting the lenses to change your vision from a blur to clarity. This clarity will help you stay true to the path God desires for you to travel without veering far from it.

Use the following guidelines to begin the process of writing a statement for your life, purpose, vision, and mission. Remember, this is a process. Start with a rough draft. Use your friends and wife, if you are married, to speak into your thinking and writing. Then keep refining your statements until they resonate with your heart.

God created you to fill a need.

• **My life purpose:** Bishop Garlington said, "Your existence preceded your conception" and "Your purpose preceded your birth." This means that God created you to fill a need. The question is, what is your unique purpose in life? Your purpose in life answers the question in your soul that wonders why you are alive and why you exist at this time in human history. These questions speak to us from the "God gene" that Bishop Garlington illustrated in his chapter. God made you for a purpose. He hardwired the questions and pursuit for purpose into your existence. And until we acknowledge this reality and answer its questions, we live frustrated lives outside the purpose for which God created us. Your life purpose is that overarching reason for your entire life.

Do not confuse your life purpose statement with your vocational assignment. Your vocational assignment will most likely change over the course of your lifetime. For example, David in the Bible had four vocational assignments: he was a shepherd, a musician, a warrior, and a king. But his overarching life purpose was to follow God with all his heart and to be a faithful leader with any assignment God commissioned to him. Remember when David wanted to build a temple for God? God said no, that He had chosen David's son Solomon to do that. David had faithfully shepherded his flock. He had faithfully played his harp for Saul. He had led the warriors of Israel in war. And he had faithfully led God's people, Israel. He would not build the temple, but he would be a legendary king of Israel.

Consider Jesus's life purpose "to seek and to save what was lost" (Luke 19:10). Everything Jesus did was in pursuit of the lost and spiritually hungry; and for those willing to believe, He freed them from spiritual and physical captivity.

So what about you? What is your life purpose statement?

Let's agree on a few givens. First, followers of Christ exist to follow Christ and to let Him lead them. So, if you are following Jesus Christ, your life will bring glory to God. Second, all followers of Christ exist to be a part of God's family—His body, or His church—and if they are doing so, they will grow in faith and mature spiritually. These are givens for anyone who professes to follow Christ.

But in addition to these givens, what is your *unique* life purpose? Look at the following life purpose statements as examples:

- "I exist to invest my life resources into other people so that they might more fully experience the risk, adventure, and freedom of a life journey with God."

- "I exist to follow my Leader, Jesus Christ, one step at a time and to strategically use my talents to optimize their influence for God's kingdom."
- "I exist to love God with all my heart, mind, strength, and soul, and to use my talents and gifts to bring physical and spiritual healing to hurting people."
- "I exist to love God, fear Him all the days of my life, and freely give to others all that God has given me so that they might discover His gift of eternal life and a life of freedom."
- "I exist to be God's son and warrior fighting for the freedom of other men's hearts."
- "I exist to follow Jesus Christ and serve His purposes by telling my life story to the next generation and encouraging them to discover their Maker."
- "I exist to love God and to love and serve people in the poorest of poor settings."
- "I exist to follow Jesus Christ and infuse His heart into America's political system."
- "I exist to use my talent to create compelling stories to tell the story of Christ and to influence the industries in which I relate."

> The words you pick should stir and rouse your passion.

What is your life purpose? The words you pick should stir and rouse your passion. You should say, "Yes! That's it. That's my life purpose." This will take time. This is deep, heart work. You will go through many edits. But start somewhere.

Beware: do not jump to the implications of your life purpose statement in this process. Some of us have a personality that quickly goes tactical or to the "how" of what a statement like this might mean for us. Going there at this point in your thinking will only pour water on the fire that God wants to ignite in you. Additionally, beware of obstacles, like the fear of finances and the fear of failure, that also hinder the discovery of your unique life purpose.

You may want to return to the discoveries of your life inventory, heart, life story, and giftedness tools in order to identify themes weaved throughout them. These insights offer clues to the right words that capture and rouse insight into your purpose.

Now write your life purpose statement in the blank space below. You will later write them in the "My Life Purpose—Vision—Mission" awakening tool. Summarize your purpose statement with a header of a few key words or a phrase inherent in your statement. Use the completed examples as a guide:

Example **My Life Purpose** (Why I Exist)	**Live Free in Christ** I exist to follow my Leader, Jesus Christ, one step at a time and to strategically optimize my talents of leadership, communication, and building to help others discover and embrace real spiritual freedom in Christ.
Example **Jesus's Life Purpose** (Why He Came to Earth)	**Seek and Save** My purpose is to seek and to save the lost. (Luke 19:10)

Your Life Purpose

My Life Purpose (Why I Exist)	

• **My life vision statement:** Bishop Garlington said, "Your believing must precede your seeing." He also said, "Vision is a living, vibrant picture of the future; it is compelling and convincing; and when you are in touch with it, you have taken a major step of faith." You cannot write your life vision statement unless you hear from God because your statement must reflect what He sees in you and your future. (You may want to reread Buddy Owens's chapter on "Hearing from God" to prime your heart and thinking.)

Ask God, "Father, what do You see in me that I don't see? What is Your vision for my life?" It's as if you are asking Him to help you hover at a high altitude over your life—with all its decades lived out—and see it as a whole. What do you see? What does He help you see? What words come to mind?

As with life purpose statements, there are some givens with life vision statements for all followers of Christ. For example, any man of God wants his heavenly Father to sum up his life with the words: "Well done, good and faithful servant!" (Matthew 25:21, 23). But why is God saying this to you in your life vision statement? That is the question you must answer.

When you think this way, it may help to envision your life as a movie film running through a projector. If you were to run the film of your life purpose statement into the future and freeze-frame it at the end of your life, what would you see? Your life vision statement is a snapshot of your entire life lived out in a way that is consistent with your life purpose statement.

Recall David's life purpose to follow God with all his heart and to be a faithful leader with any assignment God asked him to take. If we were to write his life vision statement, it might say: God's vision for David was to install him as the king of Israel forever (see 1 Chronicles 28:4). Obviously, David didn't see that or comprehend it until later in his life. But his faithfulness to his life purpose prepared him to hear and accept God's vision for him.

We said that Jesus's life purpose statement was "to seek and to save the lost." If we were to write a life vision statement for Him, we might say that His vision was to see the kingdom of God come on earth as it is in heaven (see Matthew 6:10). All that Jesus said and demonstrated tied into God's power and authority to free people spiritually and physically. It's as if Jesus was invading Satan's darkness with the light, life, and power of God's kingdom in order to establish his Father's rule and reign fully on earth—just as it is in heaven.

> Your life vision statement is a snapshot of your entire life.

What is your life vision statement? Utilize your friends and others to help you clarify it, but more than anything, get away from the noise of your life to hear from God. Here are some examples of life vision statements to stir your thinking:

- "God's vision for me is to be a man resolutely committed to a life that is free from worldly entrapment, that produces enduring benefit, and that is destined to enter into God-sourced joy and reward."
- "God's vision for my life is to reveal His existence, love, and mercy through my heart and gift to help sick people."
- "God's vision for me is to optimize my talents and influence in public policy and influence it with His thinking and values."
- "God's vision for me is to pour Christ's life in me into others, beginning with my wife and kids, and to anyone else He brings into my path through my work, church, and community."
- "God's vision for me is for me to bring a message of hope to the next generation of modern-day Israel."
- "God's vision for me is to be a spiritual father to soldiers."
- "God's vision for me is to stir the hearts of my family, my colleagues at work, friends, and any one else to see their life story as intricately connected to God's epic story."
- "God's vision for me is to have a large spiritual family tree in my older years, each of whom I've played a part in helping connect with and live for God."

Now write your life vision. Summarize it in a heading with a few words or a short phrase found within your vision statement. Use the following examples as illustrations:

Example **My Life Vision** (What God Sees in Me)	**Invest in Others** God sees me as a spiritual father to others and wants me to invest my energy, faith, talents, and experiences into others who need a mentor and guide.

Example **Jesus's Life Vision** (What He Saw)	**My Father's Kingdom** My vision is to see God's kingdom on earth as it is in heaven. (Matthew 6:10)

Your Life Vision

My Life Vision (What God Sees in Me)	

• **My life mission:** Bishop Garlington said, "Your assignment preceded your awareness." He also said, "Your mission is your assignment, and it is never optional; it is the key to your purpose and your vision. You can't ever be truly happy until you are engaged in the tasks that are accomplishing your particular mission."

What is your life mission?

David's life mission was to accept God's mantle of king and rule Israel with the fear and courage of God. He did it. Mission accomplished. Jesus's mission was to die on the cross. His last words were, "It is finished" (John 19:30). Mission accomplished.

What is your life mission? What is the mission that you must accept, pursue, and accomplish in your lifetime? Following are some example life mission statements:

- "My life mission is to step into God-directed channels of opportunity to create value and human benefit."
- "My life mission is to plant churches in unchurched places in Africa."
- "My life mission is to lead and influence corporate business culture, and those within it, with the love and truth of God."

- "My life mission is to teach the next generation about life and introduce them to Christ."
- "My life mission is to be God's messenger through journalism."
- "My life mission is to pastor God's people (starting with my own family)."
- "My life mission is to use my gift to make money by investing in high return on investment ventures and with the return help fund ministries that reach and help orphaned kids."
- "My life mission is to make movies that are crafted on biblical values and that encourage healthy families."
- "My life mission is to share my life story, and God's place in it, with the people and families God brings into my life—especially those through my legal practice."
- "My life mission is to impact young men for Christ as a coach."

Now begin to write your life mission. Revise it until you can state it in one sentence, and then attempt to summarize it with the key words or phrase.

Again, some examples are provided to spark your thinking:

Example **My Life Mission** (What I Must Do)	**Pour My Life into Third World Entrepreneurs** My mission is to use the connections I have worldwide to help the less fortunate discover and mature their God-given talent and to share my faith and story with them so they might know God, too, and help others.

Example **Jesus's Life Mission** (What He Had to Do)	**The Cross** My mission is to die on the cross for the sin of humanity. (John 19:30)

Your Life Mission

My Life Mission (What I Must Do)	

phase 2: focus

The Primary Obstacles in My Path

Bishop Garlington said that "obstacles are sure to stand in your way of living your life purpose." But, he also said, "Obstacles are opportunities."

Notice in the "My Life Purpose—Vision—Mission" awakening tool that there is a column to the right titled "Obstacles to My Life Purpose, Vision, and Mission." What are the obstacles in the path of your purpose, vision, and mission? You may be facing the fear of change or of finances or of failure. Or sin-obstacles might stand in your way: the sin of greed or sexual sin or some addiction of some kind. Many of these obstacles are within our control to begin to maneuver around or through. Other obstacles are not in our control, like the obstacles of the illness of a spouse or child or impending bankruptcy. But before you evaluate how God wants you to respond to an obstacle, you first need to identify them. Do so in the right column of the awakening tool. The completed fictional example will help you.

The Awakening Experience Process

Phase 1 **AWARENESS** *Awakening to Who I Am*	Phase 2 **FOCUS** *Awakening to God's Adventure for Me*	Phase 3 **PREPARATION** *Awakening to How I Must Live*	Phase 4 **FREEDOM** *Living the Awakened Life*
My Life in Christ **Taking Inventory** **My Heart** **My Life Story** **My Giftedness**	**My Life Purpose** **My Life Vision** **My Life Mission** ***The Primary Obstacles in My Path***	My Guiding Convictions Personal Battle Plan Family Battle Plan Work Battle Plan Church Battle Plan Community Battle Plan	Friendship Battle Plan Guides Along the Way Time Analysis Life Journey Reviews
Where Am I Now?	Where Does God Want to Take Me?	How Must I Live to Get There?	How Will I Stay the Course?

	God's Reason for Creating Me	Obstacles to My Life Purpose, Vision, and Mission
My Life Purpose (Why I Exist)		
My Life Vision (What God Sees in Me)		
My Life Mission (What I Must Do)		

My Life Purpose—Vision—Mission ▶ Fictional Example

	God's Reason for Creating Me	Obstacles to My Life Purpose, Vision, and Mission
My Life Purpose (Why I Exist)	**Live Free in Christ** I exist to follow my leader, Jesus Christ, one step at a time and to strategically optimize my talents of leadership, communication, and building to help others live free in Christ.	Money: I fear that if I were to live this way, I would not be able to continue my current way of life.
My Life Vision (What God Sees in Me)	**Invest in Others** God sees me as a spiritual father to others and wants me to invest my energy, faith, talents, and experiences into others who need a mentor and guide.	Failure: What if this doesn't work? What will others think of me?
My Life Mission (What I Must Do)	**Pour My Life into Third World Entrepreneurs** My mission is to use the connections I have worldwide to help the less fortunate discover and mature their God-given talent and to share my faith and story with them so that they might know God, too, and help others.	Sin: I am not currently in a place of total surrender and freedom and am dabbling in lust and sexual sin.

My Life Purpose—Vision—Mission ▶ Example of Jesus

	God's Reason for Creating Me	Obstacles to My Life Purpose, Vision, and Mission
My Life Purpose (Why I Exist)	**Seek and Save** My purpose is to seek and to save the lost. (Luke 19:10)	The Enemy: The enemy and his temptations (Matthew 4:1–11).
My Life Vision (What God Sees in Me)	**My Father's Kingdom** My vision is to see God's kingdom on earth as it is in heaven. (Matthew 6:10)	Temptation: The temptation to have the "cup" of the cross pass from Him (Matthew 26:42).
My Life Mission (What I Must Do)	**The Cross** My mission is to die on the cross for the sin of humanity. (John 19:30)	He was tempted in all the ways we are all tempted (Hebrews 4:15).

a word about surrender

Surrender is a vital and important component in the awakening experience. In fact, it is possible to awaken to who you are in Christ, gain clarity on your heart for life and your giftedness, and even focus on your life purpose, vision, and mission. But if you do not surrender all of who you are and why you exist to your Maker, then you will not travel the adventure and path God has for you. Surrender is simple—and it is the hardest component of following Christ. We need His help to do so. But when you surrender, you are free to live the life God has created you to live.

Surrender is waving the white flag—again—to God. Surrender involves yielding, releasing, and giving up your reputation, future, possessions, money, health, time, fears, anxieties, questions—everything—to God. Surrender is both a point in time and an ongoing reality to any follower of Christ who intends to live the adventure God has for him. A surrendered man will do whatever God asks of him and go wherever Christ leads him. A surrendered man is an instrument for God to use however He pleases.

You may want to get away for a half day, a full day, or more in order to pray about what you are discovering in this process. Sometimes we need to extract ourselves from the noise of our lives in order to hear God's voice. In doing so, we connect with our Father, resonate with what He thinks, and surrender ourselves in a new and fresh way to His pull on our lives.

With that said, and in light of where we are in this process, take some time to write a letter of surrender to God. A template and space to write this letter follows. Write to God. Be real. Be personal. This letter is from your heart to God's heart.

my complete surrender to God

Today's Date: _____

Dear Father,

Your son,

checkup

Time for a checkup. How are you progressing through the Awakening Experience Process? You have taken inventory of your life. You have discovered what God has written on your heart. You have gleaned from your life journey and its highs and lows. You have discovered your giftedness. And you have now used all the discoveries from these tools to write your life purpose, vision, and mission statements. We have now progressed through Phase 2 of the Awakening Experience Process.

The Awakening Experience Process

Phase 1 **AWARENESS** *Awakening to Who I Am*	Phase 2 **FOCUS** *Awakening to God's Adventure for Me*
My Life in Christ **Taking Inventory** **My Heart** **My Life Story** **My Giftedness**	**My Life Purpose** **My Life Vision** **My Life Mission** **The Primary Obstacles in My Path**
Where Am I Now?	Where Does God Want to Take Me?

Remind yourself and your friends that this is a process of discovery, hearing from God and updating and refining what you have been working on. Remember that the discoveries from each awakening tool build on each other. The goal is not to complete the process, but to awaken to the purpose of your life story within God's epic story. You are alive for a reason. God created you with foresight and intention. When you are able to clarify and focus why you are here on earth, then you can strategically fulfill His purpose and design for you.

You are now ready to advance to Phase 3 of the Awakening Experience Process and develop battle plans for each part of your life: personal life, home life, work life, church life, community life, and friendships. You will get more tactical and practical in living your life purpose, moving toward your life vision, and faithfully fulfilling your life mission. These battle plans are your preparation plans. You will use these plans to live the awakened life God has created you to live.

So hang in there. Encourage each other. Stir each other up. You are on a journey filled with many unpredictable surprises. But you are awakening to where you are going and how God wants you to get there.

Onward!

You can strategically fulfill His purpose and design for you.

CHAPTER 6

living the awakened life at home

Dan Seaborn

It started out innocently. I was in bed one night, watching ESPN like I usually do before I doze off. My wife and I had prayed together moments earlier, and afterward she had fallen asleep snuggled up in my arm. It was mostly quiet in our house that night; the only sound was a low murmur coming from the TV. And except for the lights of SportsCenter flickering in my bedroom, it was mostly dark in the house, too.

During one commercial break, I picked up the remote and started channel surfing. That's when I noticed our cable service was giving us a slew of free movie channels. This was a surprise, because we normally order just the TV necessities—NBA, NFL, and cartoons for the kids. So you can imagine how excited I got when I saw a bunch of extras on the screen in front of me.

I flipped through the freebies until I got to one particular channel where the camera shot was blurred and slowly coming into focus. A box at the top of my screen told me the movie was called *Basic Instinct*. I had heard that title before but had never seen the movie.

If you're a devoted film fan, you should know that I'm not one. I don't rent many videos, and if I go to a theater it's usually to pick some kids up or to drop some kids off. Most of the time, I'd rather see LeBron James or Tiger Woods playing circles around their competition. So when I stopped to watch *Basic Instinct*, I had no idea what to expect.

As the picture came into focus, though, the gist of the movie was blatantly obvious. The first clear image to hit my TV screen was a nude woman in the middle of an erotic sex scene. With that, everything changed.

Suddenly, unexpectedly, I was faced with a moment of truth: would I change the channel, or would I just keep watching? Without warning, my mind launched into a tug of war between those two options. My convictions lined up on one side of a rope, my physical desires anchored themselves on the other end, and then both teams grabbed on and heaved with all their might.

Sixty Seconds of Failure

Yeah, yeah, I hear you—an R-rated movie is hardly something most people get concerned about these days. From triple-X pay-per-views in the hotel room and peep shows along the side of the highway, a lot of guys are looking at stuff that's a whole lot worse than *Basic Instinct*, right? Sure they are. And I used to be one of them.

Some people claim to have a photographic memory; I'm convinced I've got a *pornographic* one. I saw a lot of pornography while I was in college, and now when I stumble across sexually illicit material, it seems like every single picture I looked at when I was nineteen comes right back to clear focus. I don't want to keep seeing them, but it's as if they're burned into my brain—I have to fight to *not* see them. This battle is a vicious one, and it's never limited to just a single moment or a couple TV frames. It's forever ongoing— a fight over my past and for my future.

So I wish I could tell you I switched right back to ESPN the second I saw even a hint of nudity. I didn't. In fact, my mental tug of war had to go a few more rounds in order for that to happen. Instead, I sat under the eerie blue glow of *Basic Instinct*.

There I was, a Christian man who leads a Christian organization, a Christian man who had just prayed with his wife, a Christian man a few months away from preaching holiness to thousands of other men across the nation. And yet there I was, a man watching

> This battle is a vicious one, and it's never limited to just a single moment or a couple TV frames.

something I should have flipped away from immediately, a man entertaining the sort of thoughts I should never have entertained, a man living the type of moment I would be ashamed to broadcast on the JumboTron at Promise Keepers.

Lying there, I was the picture of contradiction. I knew I should change the channel, but I couldn't bring myself to press a single button on my remote.

I wanted to win this tug of war, so I gently nudged my wife out of her sleep beside me. "Babe," I said, "we're getting a free movie channel that has something I don't need to see." It was instant accountability, and it helped. I switched back to SportsCenter.

When I turned off the TV for good that night, though, I lay in bed feeling disgusted with myself. Sure, I had stumbled on the movie. Sure, I hadn't known what the film was about. Sure, I had watched for only sixty seconds, tops. But I knew those sixty seconds mattered, because I felt like a total failure afterward.

So although I eventually stopped watching the movie and integrity won the final battle in that night's tug of war, I still didn't feel victorious. I may have pulled hard in the end, but the skin on my palms still stung with rope burn. And I had mud on my chin from what felt like one huge loss.

The Irony

Last year, for Christmas, my wife bought me an official NFL football autographed by the Detroit Lions' Hall of Fame running back Barry Sanders. From the moment I lifted that ball out of its box, I didn't want anyone else to touch it. It didn't matter to me that the Lions haven't been NFL champs since 1957; I still didn't want anybody to put their grimy hands on that ball. As soon my favorite hobby store opened on the day after Christmas, I was there, picking out a protective case for my Barry ball.

Here's the irony of Dan Seaborn: I shelter a piece of sports equipment with the most excellent care—perched on the highest

shelf, in an acrylic case—yet I leave aspects of my home vulnerable to dangerous elements like lust. I lock the front door of my house to keep all of my stuff safe, but I also swung wide the doors of *Basic Instinct*. I can be more focused in guarding a scrap of leather against fingerprints than I can be in defending myself and my family against sin.

"I do not understand what I do," Paul wrote to the Romans. "For what I want to do I do not do, but what I hate I do" (Romans 7:15). I'm no apostle, but I can definitely relate to that feeling.

A Battle for All the Marbles

Of all the places where a man needs to live the awakened life, it's most important that he lives the awakened life in his own home. The person he is behind his own front door determines the person he becomes when he walks out that door. The decisions he makes and the actions he takes under his own roof set in motion his decisions and actions everywhere else.

In other words, if you want to live the awakened life at all, you have to start by living it where it really counts—at home.

If you're a husband or a father or both, your responsibility to live an awakened home life can feel doubly intense, because your decisions at home directly affect other people on a daily basis. While that's true, it doesn't mean single guys and sons who live with their parents are off the hook. God expects *all* of our homes to be a reflection of Himself.

Here's how I know that: throughout the Bible, the relationship between a husband and a wife is paralleled to the relationship between Christ and His church. That's one powerful comparison—it says a lot about the significance of marriage. But there's more to it than just that. The Bible's plan for a family is that it should begin with marriage. So the fact that God's Word compares husbands and wives to Christ and the church is telling us a whole lot about family. It's telling us God puts utmost importance on family life

God expects *all* of our homes to be a reflection of Himself.

and that God wants our homes here on earth to be what I call a replica of heaven.

Here's the problem: Satan would like for our homes to be a replica of hell instead. He knows that what happens in our homes has the potential to point others toward Christ, and he will do anything to destroy that. He'll ambush you by whatever means possible—through cheating, gossip, alcohol and drug abuse, the Internet, and even free movie channels.

This really is an epic battle, you see, because the stakes are higher in this battle than in any other. There's a trickle-down effect: the way you behave at home eventually affects all the others around you. So it's a huge risk to be asleep to temptations and sins that threaten your home, because this one's for all the marbles. To lose here is to lose completely. But to live the awakened life at home—to *win* at home—is to win all.

Carrying the Tools at Home

The Bible says, "Unless the Lord builds the house, its builders labor in vain" (Psalm 127:1). I'd like you to pay attention to the fact that this verse identifies the Lord as the builder and us as the builders. So it's a team thing—God is the master builder, and we're the laborer builders. He's got the plan, and we carry the tools.

Our job as men is to follow His blueprint and keep ourselves at His fingertips. Then He can do good work both in and through us.

So how can we stay at His fingertips? Here's a start:

Wake up to the obvious. Stop hitting the snooze button on changes you should be making right now. Take action, and change them. Paul writes in Romans, "Those who live according to the sinful nature have their minds set on what that nature desires; but those who live in accordance with the Spirit have their minds set on what the Spirit desires" (8:5). In other words, if Christ has revealed areas you need to adjust in your home life—your patience with your children, your

attitude toward your wife, your habits—be obedient to what you already know and allow the Spirit to change you.

Take a step of humility. Die to self. Sacrifice some of the rights you think you deserve. This will require saying no to some things that might normally get your time, but—I guarantee it—a servant attitude will change your home like nothing else can.

Be honest. Let people see and know the true you. Pride keeps many of us from saying, "I struggle" or, "I'm not perfect" or, "Pray for me." We have tricked ourselves into believing that if we tell others what we're really like, they'll banish us to the desert. That's just not true; people would rather have honesty than false flawlessness.

Develop accountability. It's easier to stay on track with somebody covering your back. Find someone who will encourage you while holding you accountable in the areas you want to grow. Have them ask you:

1. How are you growing spiritually?
2. What have you learned from the Bible this week?
3. Are you keeping your thoughts pure?
4. Have you done anything that would jeopardize your integrity?
5. Have you done anything that would jeopardize your family?

Humble yourself and find somebody who will make you face up to your behaviors.

Seek the Lord. Study the Bible, pray, and listen for the Lord's voice. Ask Him to reveal areas of sin in your life at home, and when He does, change. Do you need to offer or request forgiveness, adjust your attitude, or correct a behavior? "Search me, O God," wrote the psalmist, "and know my heart.... See if there is any offensive way in me" (139:23–24). In short, ask God to give you a wake-up call.

An awakened home life is the best thing you could build in your life. It's worth every effort you could put into it—first tries, second tries, even failed tries. And, trust me, it's worth changing the channel.

> Be obedient to what you already know and allow the Spirit to change you.

phase 3: preparation

My Guiding Convictions

Don't you love it when men are honest about their humanity and their need for God? That's what Dan Seaborn just did in his chapter. As men who want to follow Christ in our own worlds—whatever those worlds might look like—we face the temptation to sin and drift from God. When we do, we sear our souls, hurt God's heart, offend other people, and make mistakes of all kinds. It's an ongoing tug of war between the dark side and our new spiritual heart—just as Dan vividly portrayed.

The question we now ask is, how are we going to fight these battles in our heads, hearts, and homes? The battles are real. The enemy is real. Is it possible to learn how the enemy attacks, respond defensively and offensively, and grow in wisdom and skill in this battle with darkness and sin?

It is possible. But to do so, you must prepare to live and fight this way. This is just the way it works in life: know where you are going, have a plan to get there, and then work and live the plan. Athletes do this. Businessmen do this. Professionals do this. Military leaders do this. Great leaders of the faith do this. And if we are going to live the awakened life God has created us to live, then we must learn to *prepare* to do so—in all the different spheres of our life.

Note where we are in the Awakening Experience Process: we have completed Phases 1 and 2 and are moving into Phase 3. By now you have taken an in-depth inventory of your life, gained clarity into what God has written on your heart, and discovered critical insights into your life story and giftedness. You have awakened to who you are in Christ.

In Phase 2, you wrote your life purpose, vision, and mission statements and awakened to what God sees in you and what you must do to get there. You also identified some of the key obstacles in your way. Though you will continue to edit, refine, and focus those statements, you are gaining clarity on why you are alive and what you must do in your lifetime.

The Awakening Experience Process

Phase 1 **AWARENESS** *Awakening to Who I Am*	Phase 2 **FOCUS** *Awakening to God's Adventure for Me*	Phase 3 **PREPARATION** *Awakening to How I Must Live*	Phase 4 **FREEDOM** *Living the Awakened Life*
My Life in Christ **Taking Inventory** **My Heart** **My Life Story** **My Giftedness**	**My Life Purpose** **My Life Vision** **My Life Mission** **The Primary Obstacles in My Path**	***My Guiding Convictions*** Personal Battle Plan Home Battle Plan Work Battle Plan Church Battle Plan Community Battle Plan	Friendship Battle Plan Guides Along the Way Time Analysis Life Journey Reviews
Where Am I Now?	Where Does God Want to Take Me?	How Must I Live to Get There?	How Will I Stay the Course?

Now you are entering Phase 3: awakening to how you must live. All of the perspective and insight gained in Phases 1 and 2 will help you identify how to move forward in living the life God created you to live. We only have so much time in a given day, week, month, year, and in the decades God allows us to live. We can't change the time factor. But we can steward it. We can live strategically within it. We can discover why we were created within time and space and then live that life.

Now, it's time to *prepare* to do so. You will begin by creating a list of your guiding convictions—your core values that govern how you engage life. They guide you. Even when you violate a core conviction, you feel guilty until you deal with it. Your guiding convictions speak to you from your conscience and spiritual heart. From them you learn to love and pursue what is good and distaste and turn from what is wrong and evil.

If you work for a company, then it most likely has a core value statement. Many large retail centers hang their core value statements on walls for customers to view. (Many churches do the same.) Organizations that intentionally impress their core values into the way their employees serve stand heads above their competitors. Core values are meant to guide the way a company does and does not do business.

Our personal core values should guide our life in the same way. That is why we are calling them "My Guiding Convictions" in the Awakening Experience Process. Like riverbanks that direct moving water through terrain of all kinds until it reaches its destination, your core convictions—when imprinted on your brain and heart—help guide the way you think, live, and relate. If you learn to listen to and respond to your guiding convictions, they will help you survive the unpredictable challenges of your life journey.

As Dan mentioned, none of us is flawless; so even when we violate our personal core values, our conscience and God's Spirit within us invoke conviction and guilt. When convicted, our core values steer us back to the path God wants us to travel.

In the following awakening tool, you will write your guiding convictions. Allow the following questions applied to each sphere of life to stir your thinking:

• **What are the guiding convictions for your personal life?** How will God's thoughts and feelings guide your thinking, living, and relating? How will you tap into the wisdom and truth of His written Word and His Spirit when you need to make a critical decision? For example, you might say, "I am committed to ask God, 'Father, what do You think about _____?' when I face critical decisions." (And fill in the blank.)

How will you respond to people when they offend you or sin against you? For example, you might say, "I am committed to forgive others when they wrong me and to ask for forgiveness when I am wrong."

When tempted to do what you know is wrong, unhealthy, or dark, how do you respond in order to live in the light and freedom of Christ? For example, you might say, "I am committed to bring darkness and struggle in my life into the light—with God and those who love me and who cover me in grace and mercy and love."

Now write your own guiding conviction statements for your personal life. Use the example below as a guide.

Guiding Convictions for My Personal Life	• • • •

Fictional Example **Guiding Convictions for My Personal Life**	• My spiritual heart needs spiritual food and exercise, and I'm committed to keep it healthy. • I'm committed to ask God what He thinks in regard to the decisions I face in my life. • When I sin or mess up, I'm committed to come clean and confess to those I sinned against. • I'm committed to forgive others when they sin against me. • My body is God's, and I am committed to take care of it.

• **What are the guiding convictions for your home life?** What are the critical, nonnegotiable, and foundational values that you want to see in your home? For example, you may be committed to honor each other and each other's things in your home since our "stuff" oftentimes incites conflict. Or you may decide to lead others in your home to reconcile by asking for and receiving forgiveness.

If you are married, will you pursue the heart of your wife creatively and consistently? Will you be committed to listen to her heart, hear her dreams, and encourage her spiritual growth?

If you have kids, will you pursue their hearts as they grow and change? Will you guide them or push them? Will you badger them or put courage into them (which is what encouragement is)? Will you be committed to instruct them, share life with them, and help them discover and live the life God desires for them?

Now write your guiding convictions for your family in the space below and use the example as an illustration:

Guiding Convictions for My Home Life	• • • •

| *Fictional Example*
 Guiding Convictions for My Home Life | • We're committed to honor God, each other, and each other's things in our home.
 • We're committed to reconcile with each other when we offend each other.
 • I'm committed to do all I can to keep the spiritual enemy from infiltrating our home.
 • I will stay honest and open with Lauren about what is going on in my head and heart.
 • I won't sacrifice my family for any other spheres of life. |

• **What are the guiding convictions for your work life?** Will you work? Will you work hard? Will you commit to excellence and mastering your work skills? Will you relate to others honestly and with love in your workplace? Will you commit to integrity in your thinking and in the way you operate and communicate?

Will you demonstrate God's role in your life in the way you work and how you relate to others through your work? Will you freely and naturally tell your life story, and God's primary role in it, when others inquire about it?

Now write your guiding convictions for your work life in the space below and use the example as an illustration:

Guiding Convictions for My Work Life	• • • •

Fictional Example **Guiding Convictions for My Work Life**	• I will work hard when its time to work and go home when its time to go home. • I'm committed not to burn bridges. • I'm committed to do my work with integrity and excellence. • I will let the actions of my work life exemplify my faith in Christ and share my life story when asked.

• **What are the guiding convictions for your church life?** Will you honor and respect the pastors God has placed in your life? Will you use your natural talents and spiritual gifts to encourage your church family? Will you be a unifier and reconciler in the body of Christ?

Now write your guiding convictions for your church life in the space below and use the example as an illustration:

Guiding Convictions for My Church Life	• • • •

Fictional Example **Guiding Convictions for My Church Life**	• I'm committed to pray for my pastor and our church leadership. • I'm committed to promote unity in the church and do all I can to unify the body of Christ. • I'm committed to invest my talents and gifts in my local church.

• **What are the guiding convictions for your community life?** Will you be open to engage, relate to, and pray for nonbelievers in your life? Will you be committed to allow God to use you as one of His instruments on earth to illustrate His love for all people? Will you be open to invest your time, talent, and treasure into the expansion of His kingdom on earth?

Now write your guiding convictions for your community life in the space below and use the example as an illustration:

Guiding Convictions for My Community Life	•
	•
	•
	•

Fictional Example **Guiding Convictions for My Community Life**	• I'm committed to pray for my neighbors and respond to real needs that they face.
	• I'm committed to mentor younger, third world entrepreneurs.
	• I'm committed to coach my son's soccer team and help the fatherless kids on my team.

• **What are the guiding convictions for your friendships?** Will you take the risk to open your life fully to a few other brothers in Christ? Will you cover them in their battles with the enemy and darkness? Will you pray for your friends and posture your heart to encourage them and stir them up to live the life God has for them?

Now write your guiding convictions for your friendships in the space below and use the example as an illustration:

Guiding Convictions for My Friendships	•
	•
	•
	•

Fictional Example **Guiding Convictions** **for My Friendships**	• I'm committed to relate deeply to Steve and Tim and to not allow the enemy of my heart to lure me and keep me in darkness and secrecy. I'm committed to encourage them in their walks with God too.

You will want to edit and rework your guiding convictions as you experience new realities. Remember, the purpose of these tools is not to complete an exercise. Rather, you are discovering how to live the life God wants and envisions for you. So give yourself freedom (and grace) to start where you are, and understand that He will help you refine your convictions.

Now insert all of your guiding convictions on the comprehensive "My Guiding Convictions" awakening tool. Put those values that apply to all life spheres in the left column and those that apply to a specific sphere in the right column. Use the example as an illustration.

Guiding Convictions for All Spheres of My Life	Specific Life Sphere Guiding Convictions
	Personal Life
	Home Life
	Work Life
	Church Life
	Community Life
	Friendships

my guiding convictions ▶ Fictional Example
Awakening to God's Core Values for Me

Guiding Convictions for All Spheres of My Life	Specific Life Sphere Guiding Convictions
	Personal Life
• I'm committed to ask God what He thinks in regard to the decisions I face in my life.	My spiritual heart needs spiritual food and exercise, and I'm committed to keep it healthy. I'm committed to ask God what He thinks in regard to the decisions I face in my life. I'm committed to forgive others when they sin against me. My body is God's, and I am committed to take care of it.
	Home Life
• When I sin or mess up, I'm committed to come clean and confess to those I sinned against.	We're committed to honor God, each other, and each other's things in our home. We're committed to reconcile with each other when we offend each other. I'm committed to do all I can to keep the spiritual enemy from infiltrating our home. I will stay honest and open with Lauren about what is going on in my head and heart. I won't sacrifice my family for any other spheres of life.
	Work Life
• I'm committed to forgive others when they sin against me.	I will work hard when its time to work and go home when its time to go home. I'm committed to not burn bridges. I'm committed to do my work with integrity and excellence. I will let the actions of my work life exemplify my faith in Christ and spare my life story when asked
• I'm committed to share my life story and God's primary role in my life story with anyone who wants to listen.	
	Church Life
	I'm committed to pray for my pastor and our church leadership. I'm committed to promote unity in the church and do all I can to unify the body of Christ. I'm committed to invest my talents and gifts in my local church.
• I'm committed to freely give away all that God has given me to others who are in need.	
	Community Life
	I'm committed to pray for my neighbors and respond to real needs that they face. I'm committed to mentor younger, third world entrepreneurs. I'm committed to coach my son's soccer team and help the fatherless kids on my team.
• I'm committed to live openly and honestly about my relationship with Christ and to avoid becoming a religious person.	
	Friendships
	I'm committed to relate deeply to Steve and Tim and to not allow the enemy of my heart to lure me and keep me in darkness and secrecy. I'm committed to encourage them in their walks with God too.

phase 3: preparation

My Personal Battle Plan

How did it go writing your guiding convictions? Do they feel right for *you*? When you read them, they should resonate with all your other discoveries in the awakening process.

Again, like other statements you have written in this process, you will want to refine your guiding convictions, simplify them, and reword them in such a way that they are progressively branded onto your brain and heart. As you use these guiding convictions to steer you through the unpredictable realities of your future, you will discover how Christ's presence in your life will help you filter the way you think, live, and relate.

It is now time to get very practical—to land the rubber on the road of your life. When we think of a flying-plane analogy, we started the awakening process from thirty thousand feet. We took assessment of our life: we looked at our heart, our life story, and our giftedness. Then we used that insight to develop our life purpose, vision, and mission statements. With each insight, we descended in altitude. All of these tools were strategic and helped us awaken to who we are and where God wants us to venture in this journey called life. Now we must prepare to live that life—to land the figurative aircraft of our lives on the runway and go for it.

We've also been using the metaphors of adventure and battle throughout this process. That's because life is a journey filled with unpredictable adventure, and it is a battle—a battle within and a battle around us. So we need to be battle-ready in the adventure called life.

You will now develop battle plans for each sphere of your life. Your battle plans will be action oriented—strategic and tactical. Every component of your battle plans will help you live your life purpose, vision, and mission. You will use all of your discoveries in

> We need to be battle-ready in the adventure called life.

Phases 1 and 2 to help you discern what you must do and become in order to live the life God created you to live. You will quantify the projected time you plan to invest in everything you do and learn to strategically steward your activity accordingly—so that you might faithfully fulfill your purpose on earth.

We'll start with your personal life. What is your personal life? It is your life apart from your wife and kids (if you are married and have children), work, church, community, and friends. Your personal life includes your spiritual, physical, sexual, and mental, and emotional self. Remember in chapter 1 that you took an in-depth inventory, or assessment, of your personal life and identified areas in which you were awake, in a slumber, asleep, and comatose. Take some time and review what you identified in this inventory and what you listed as primary issues to address. You may need to update your inventory.

Now review all of your discoveries in Phase 1 of the Awakening Experience Process. Look at what you discovered in the "My Heart" awakening tool. Review your life story discoveries. Look at your giftedness summary. Then review your life purpose, vision, and mission statements from Phase 2. Look at the obstacles in your way and review your core values. Look at your guiding convictions for your personal life that you recently wrote. As you go through each completed tool in the Awakening Experience Process, identify anything that impacts and affects how you should live in your personal sphere of life.

In addition to the completed example, use the following guidelines to help you write your personal life battle plan:

• **Personal life goals:** Goals are measurable. You know when you have accomplished a goal. You might measure a goal with time, a completed project or activity within that time, or even with another quantifier like money. In regard to your personal life, you might set a goal to work out physically a minimum of three times a week, thirty

minutes per workout. Or you might set a goal to burn 3,500 calories per week. Spiritually, you might set a goal to study the words of Jesus for twenty minutes a day and journal your reflections and prayers in response to His words. Or your might set aside a half day a week to go to the mountains or beach to walk, pray, think, and personally refuel. Think about your spiritual, physical, sexual, financial, mental, and emotional life and list the things that you want to start doing and becoming. These are your personal life goals.

• **Current status:** On a scale of 1 to 3, list the current status of each goal. Let "1" symbolize a thumbs-up status (👍), "2" a mediocre or thumbs-sideways status (✊), and "3" a thumbs-down status (👎). For example, let's say you make it a goal to take a half day a month to go to the beach in order to read, pray, and reflect. If you are currently doing that, give yourself a "1" or thumbs-up. If you do it but do it irregularly, then give yourself a "2" or sideways thumb. (If you are downloading these awakening tools at **www.promisekeepers.org/AwakeningExperience**, then you can download these thumb icons and use them in the current status column. Otherwise, use a number 1, 2, or 3.)

• **Action steps:** Every goal will have a series of action steps. Action steps are tactical details that need to be systematically accomplished in order for you to progress toward accomplishing a certain goal. If you want to take a half day off each month in order to go to the beach to read and reflect, you may need to clear that day during the week or on the a weekend. If it's on the weekend and you are married and have kids, then you will want to discuss this with your wife and make sure that both of you are in agreement. Or perhaps she will want to go with you and read and refuel herself. List all the action steps needed to help you move toward accomplishing your goal.

• **By?:** Each action step should have a deliverable date attached to it. If you have a goal to get out of all nonmortgage debt in the next three years, then you will need to systematically plan the

Be encouraged. You are getting very strategic and tactical.

steps to accomplish that goal. Perhaps you will pay off a credit card by a certain date. Then you may plan to pay off your car debt by another date. And so on. Think through a realistic time line for each action step.

• **Projected time per month:** Figure out how much time you will invest in a goal per month by attaching projected time to the appropriate action steps. For example, if you make it a goal to exercise for thirty minutes, three times a week, then you would multiply 1.5 hours by 4.33 weeks per month for a total of six hours a month.

Use the completed example as an illustration, and ask your friends and/or wife to help you identify goals that will move your personal life toward health, balance, and living the life God desires you to live. Remember: this is the first of six battle plans that you will develop (see Phases 3 and 4 of the Awakening Experience Process). At the end of this process, we will perform a time analysis on all six battle plans—to see if you actually have the time in your life to do and live all that you mapped out. So don't be derailed by the total amount of time in your personal life battle plan.

For example, the illustrated personal battle plan indicates that this fictional man plans to invest forty-seven hours a month into his personal life. If you are married and have kids, you might think, *There's no way I can give that much time to my personal life.* And you might be right. Don't go there right now. When you perform a time analysis at the end of the Awakening Experience Process, you will discover if you have that kind of time for your personal life. For now, let your battle plan and the projected time be what it is.

Be encouraged. You are getting very strategic and tactical. You can always change what you have crafted. This is a *process*—a process of discovery and adventure. Enjoy the ride!

Personal Life Goals	Current Status? (1-3)	Action Steps	By?	Projected Time per Month	Notes
1.					
2.					
3.					
4.					
5.					

Total Hours per Month

my personal battle plan ➤ Fictional Example
Awakening to God's Adventure for Me

Personal Life Goals	Current Status? (1-3)	Action Steps	By?	Projected Time per Month	Notes
1. To be connected to God in such a way that I am regularly hearing Him and feeding my mind and spirit with His truth and life.	(2) 👎	a. Begin to read the Sermon on the Mount for depth, not for distance.	4/15	10	I'll start by setting aside 20 minutes a day and see how it goes.
		b. Take the morning of the fourth Thursday every month to get away, read, reflect, write.	5/1	17	I need to tell my secretary about this.
2. To be caring for my body through regular exercise and healthier eating and to weigh 195 by the end of the year.	(3) 👆	a. Discover and start a workout plan in my local recreation center.	5/15	6	I want to see if Lauren would like to do this with me.
		b. Talk to Jim about his nutrition program and start doing it.	5/15	N/A	
3. Stay out of all nonmortgage debt and pay off our house loan in the next eight years.	(1) ✋	a. Keep our current budgeting and debt payment schedule that we have been using.	Ongoing	5	Stay connected and communicating with Lauren about our finances.
4. Set up the appropriate accountability structure so I don't dabble in sexual temptation and sin.	(3) 👆	a. Move toward opening up with Lauren about my struggles.	4/15	N/A	I'm tired of fighting this battle alone and need to open up with others and bring this into the light.
		b. Let Steve and Tim into my battle with lust.	4/10	N/A	
		c. Put a filter on my home Internet system.	4/8	1 hr. 1x	
5. Start designing and building wood furniture in my wood shop again as a healthy, enjoyable outlet.	(2) 👎	a. Clean out the storage boxes from my work area.	4/15	2 hrs. 1x	Lauren has been wanting me to make a new bunk bed for the kids.
		b. Spend a couple of hours each week designing and creating.	5/1	9	

Total Hours per Month   **47**

phase 3: preparation

My Home Battle Plan

Dan Seaborn encouraged us to wake up to the obvious in our homes. This applies to married men, men with kids, and single men. All of us need a battle plan for our home front. Our battle plan should guide us toward doing and becoming what God wants us to do and become at home. It should guide us toward investing in the relationships in our home. If we are married, it should help us pursue—in creative and ongoing ways—the heart of our wife. If we have kids, it should guide us to do the same with them. If we have housemates of some kind, it should help us live in peace and health. Or it may guide us toward reconciling with a parent or sibling, or connecting with another extended family member.

We will use the same format for your home battle plan that we used for your personal battle plan. Again, use the completed example to help you think creatively and guide you toward application that is unique to you. Don't forget to review your family inventory assessment from chapter 1 and all your discoveries in Phases 1 and 2 that apply to your home life.

Be encouraged. You are crafting a battle plan for your home front. The enemy of your heart does not like you to pray, reflect, think, and plan this way. You are awakening to how God created you and how He desires for you to live. It's an entirely new way of strategically investing your time and energy in things and people. So ask God how He wants you to live and relate in your home and family—and enjoy the adventure and process! Don't forget to encourage each other to do the same. Use the fictional example as a guide.

Remember, we will integrate and review all of your battle plans at the end of the process, including a time analysis. Don't worry about your projected time for now.

> The enemy of your heart does not like you to pray, reflect, think, and plan this way.

my home battle plan
Awakening to God's Adventure for Me

Family Life Goals	Current Status? (1-3)	Action Steps	By?	Projected Time per Month	Notes
1.					
2.					
3.					
4.					
5.					

Total Hours per Month

	Family Life Goals	Current Status? (1-3)	Action Steps	By?	Projected Time per Month	Notes
1.	To be creatively and ongoingly pursuing Lauren's heart so she knows, without a doubt, that I love her and am hers.	(2) 👎	a. To plan and follow through on dating Lauren twice a month.	4/15	8	I'll even get the baby-sitter.
			b. To plan and follow through on two three-day-long getaways, one in the spring and one in the fall.	5/1	8	No kids on these.
2.	To be connected to my kids as they grow up, by pursuing them, engaging their world, and encouraging them.	(2) 👎	a. Date Jenny once a month.	5/15	2	Just the two of us at a time. Like relational "drops in a bucket."
			b. Date Jake once a month.	5/15	3	
3.	Organize and plan annual family vacations with Lauren.	(1) 👉	a. Get these on our annual calendars in January each year.	Ongoing	N/A	Going to Vancouver this July and Mexico next year.
4.	To be connected, fully reconciled, and encouraging to our parents as they enter their elderly years.	(3) 👍	a. Write a letter to my deceased dad and work with my pastor to fully forgive him and move on.	6/1	N/A	Dad did the best he could with what he had. I just need to forgive him and move on, but I need help.
			b. See our moms every Christmas in Arizona.	12/31	Seasonal	
5.	Organize an annual hunting trip with my brothers and all of our sons.	(2) 👎	a. Talk to Bryan and Chip.	4/15	N/A	We did this last year. Why not make it
			b. Plan on Montana this year.	10/1	Seasonal	a spiritual rite of passage experience?

Total Hours per Month	22

checkup

How are you doing in the Awakening Experience Process? You are advancing. Are you helping your friends do the same? Are you letting others who love you and know you into your thinking and planning?

You are now discovering how you can invest your time and energy to fulfill your life purpose, vision, and mission. You are learning to apply your giftedness and heart to real people in real spheres in your life. By now you have completed your personal and home battle plans. You are in Phase 3 in the Awakening Experience Process—preparing for how you can live the awakened life.

The Awakening Experience Process

Phase 1 **AWARENESS** *Awakening to Who I Am*	Phase 2 **FOCUS** *Awakening to God's Adventure for Me*	Phase 3 **PREPARATION** *Awakening to How I Must Live*	Phase 4 **FREEDOM** *Living the Awakened Life*
My Life in Christ **Taking Inventory** **My Heart** **My Life Story** **My Giftedness**	**My Life Purpose** **My Life Vision** **My Life Mission** **The Primary Obstacles in My Path**	***My Guiding Convictions*** ***Personal Battle Plan*** ***Home Battle Plan*** Work Battle Plan Church Battle Plan Community Battle Plan	Friendship Battle Plan Guides Along the Way Time Analysis Life Journey Reviews
Where Am I Now?	Where Does God Want to Take Me?	How Must I Live to Get There?	How Will I Stay the Course?

Your battle plans will give you a sense of how to engage the enemy of your life and heart in the different spheres of your life. But, as with any conflict, there are surprises in battles. Unexpected and unpredictable things happen that we could not foresee. Consequently, you will need to adjust and update your battle plans to take these realities into account. Please download the awakening tools at **www.promisekeepers.org/AwakeningExperience** and keep them in a useable format in your computer or with fresh printouts.

In the next chapter, Dr. Bob Reccord will help you think about your work life. It is the sphere of your life where you spend the most waking hours. But are you living the awakened life at work? That's the question we must all face.

Be encouraged. Stir each other up in your men's group. Keep each other in the game. You are advancing. You are discovering and creating a plan to live alert and awake to God and the battle. You are forging a life story that is intricately connected to His epic story, and your role in God's story is essential. Take one step at a time. Keep your spiritual senses alert to God's thinking and input and guidance. Go in faith . . . and courage.

Onward!

Your battle plans will give you a sense of how to engage the enemy of your life and heart.

▶living the awakened life at work

Bob Reccord, PhD

I'm a construction worker, and I don't see any way God can be concerned about my job.

As a follower of Christ, I feel my work in sales is sort of second rate. To have an eternally significant job, I'd need to go into full-time ministry or missions.

I know preachers and missionaries are called, but guys like me in the business and professional world have to settle for a career. I remember wondering if God would ever call me to do something for Him . . . but I never felt seminary was my thing.

I'm amazed at the impact people in full-time Christian service can have. But I'm just a layman trying to do the best I can.

I've heard these and similar statements many times. Over the years an artificial gulf has developed that seems to separate clergy and laity, secular and sacred, ministry and the marketplace. Even more damaging is the impression that "full-time Christian service" requires heading off to seminary or the mission field.

It's time for a radical adjustment in men's hearts and minds. Without question, we need to maintain the high honor of God's call to vocational missions and ministry. God does call pastors and missionaries to equip *all* of us who are Christ followers, so we can do the work of the ministry and as a result change our world (see Ephesians 4:11–12).

But we also need to expand our view of *calling* to apply to all people of God in the workplace. That's where the church can have—and, frankly, has *always* had—some of its greatest impact.

The Bible's Hall of Fame

Hebrews 11 lists what we popularly call the "Hall of Fame of Faith." Note the names of the heroes of faith God used throughout biblical history to change their world. Then ask yourself, how many of these people were priests and prophets? It's hard to believe, isn't it? If you don't think you're right, go back and read Hebrews 11 again. You were probably correct the first time!

Only one was a priest or prophet—Samuel. Although others are described with the simple words "and the prophets," pay attention to those heroes of the faith who made such an impact that their names were actually listed. Does it amaze you that the rest were herdsmen, builders, military leaders, government leaders, statesmen, pioneers, and so on? And not all of them had stellar pasts.

Do you find it interesting that when Jesus called His twelve apostles, He didn't go to the temple and call twelve priests? Instead, He went to the marketplace and called twelve workingmen in occupations we can understand today. Jesus needed their skills! He chose them to follow Him and to invest their lives for three and a half years so that—as a result of their relationship together—they could change their world.

It's time that we, the men of this generation, awaken to the fact that God has called us to the workplace to help change the world right where we are. That's why I wrote a book on this subject entitled *Made to Count* (W Publishing, 2004)—because the workplace is where most of us spend our time. God created you to flesh out His calling and purpose for your life and to be a world changer whether you're a software developer or a plumber or a dentist or a farmer or a network manager or a welder or a graphic artist or a technician or . . . well, you get the picture. And His challenge to you is much greater than merely settling into a career. Like He did for the people named in Hebrews 11, God wants you to fulfill a calling.

> God has called us to the workplace to help change the world right where we are.

How My Thinking Changed

After committing to follow Christ and having gone to Indiana University to study medicine, the course of my journey radically changed. I went to seminary. There I was taught the celebration of "the call," something that seemed to apply only to people in vocational ministry and missions. I guess I saw two categories: "the called" and, well, "the un-called." It's embarrassing to admit, but I was unintentionally buying into a dual-class system that was reinforced by everyone around me.

After a while, I began to question that point of view. I noticed that people in the church applauded with an overwhelming voice of affirmation when someone announced their "call" to the ministry or the mission field. But my study of Scripture and my understanding of the world around me changed my thinking.

Of course, the church should celebrate when someone realizes "God wants me in the ministry" or "I'm called to the mission field." But why wouldn't the church respond just as enthusiastically when people recognize that their gift for science is God-given or their natural interest in how things are put together equips them to be a mechanic or an engineer? Couldn't our culture use more doctors who believe every human life is sacred? Couldn't we use more men who repair cars or build bridges as if people's lives depended on their work?

What about work that's done with such excellence that it glorifies God? Can a forklift operator be so filled with the Holy Spirit that his enthusiasm spills out to co-workers? Can an accountant be so interested in the well-being of his clients that they see Christ in his attitude?

In fact, the more I matured, the more I realized that raising a family is a calling from God and that He even calls some people to retire from one occupation when they feel they can afford it to devote more time to ministry-related pursuits. So a systems analyst and his homemaker wife with a healthy 401(k) and an empty nest

may choose to downsize and live on a part-time consulting income so they can spend more time helping start churches.

Three Men Who "Got" It

Three men helped me crystallize this more balanced biblical understanding of being *on mission* in their occupations—that is, having an intentional and deliberate lifestyle of serving God with excellence and introducing others to Him as they go about their work.

Campbell Dow was a successful insurance salesman. But I noticed he wasn't just about insurance sales. Yes, he cared for his clients' needs for financial security. But I also knew him to say, "Now that I've been able to help with your financial needs, would you mind if we discuss your spiritual needs?" As a result, Campbell led people to Christ as a natural outgrowth of his role as their insurance agent. He'd discovered his most effective role—as a *minister on mission*.

Paul Teague was a successful businessman. He was chairman of the deacons at the church I first served. I watched Paul's amazing skill at leading people in his company, building them into successes using biblical principles. What he did at work, he transferred to his role at church. Finally I asked him to mentor me in leadership. He replied, "I'll be thrilled to mentor you in leadership, if you will in turn mentor me in discipleship." Thus began a journey of love and growth between a twenty-four-year-old seminary graduate and a forty-four-year-old *entrepreneur on mission*.

J. T. Williams soon crossed my path. He was a land developer and builder in Florida. His dad had been mayor of Tallahassee while J. T. was growing up, and the family was active in church. As a boy, J. T. sensed God doing something in his life, stirring his heart to serve Him. One day he knocked on his pastor's door. When the pastor appeared, J. T. explained what was happening in his heart. "I know God's doing something in me, so I guess I need to get ready to be a preacher and go to seminary."

They carried out their ministry in secular occupations.

"Why do you feel that way?" the pastor asked.

"Because that's what you do when God is working in your life, I guess."

The pastor asked J. T. what he was passionate about and what he thought he would love to do when he grew up. J. T. talked about watching his dad's career as a mayor, businessman, and politician impact the lives of so many. "I'd really love to do that, but I guess I need to go to seminary."

Wisely, the pastor counseled J. T. to prayerfully consider his passions and what work would really provide his sense of fulfillment. J. T. became convinced that his destination was not seminary but the marketplace. Perhaps he could reach more who would never darken the doors of the church than he could by going the seminary route. His pastor enthusiastically affirmed his decision and launched J. T. into becoming a *public servant on mission*.

As the years passed, J. T. touched the lives of government leaders not only by building their homes, but eventually as chairman of the Governor's Prayer Breakfast. His professional path was not always easy, yet God used the hard times too. When J. T. experienced bankruptcy, his business partner accepted Christ because of the steadfastness he saw in J. T.'s trust in God even when the bottom dropped out.

These three men greatly impacted my view of God's calling. I saw fleshed out in their lives just as strong a sense of call to being *on mission* as I saw in the lives of pastors and missionaries. They carried out their ministry in secular occupations. They also worked hand in hand with their pastor to impact their community and to send missionaries to lost people in North America and around the world.

God's View of Your Work

Did you know that...

- Of Jesus's 132 public appearances in the New Testament, 122 were in the marketplace?
- Of 52 parables Jesus told, 45 had a workplace context?
- Of 40 divine interventions recorded in Acts, 39 were in the marketplace?
- Jesus spent more than 50 percent of His life as a carpenter before he went into a preaching ministry in the workplace?
- Jesus called 12 workplace individuals, not clergy, to build His church?

We don't have to look further than the creation story to discover God's high view of productivity and the fulfillment the first man and woman would experience by carrying out the work He assigned to them. Throughout Scripture, God called people to follow Him and change their world. That calling has come as a twofold summons: a call to a *personal relationship with God* and a call to a *purposeful mission alongside God*. This second calling is to a specific role, joining Him in being *on mission* to change the world and to bring it back to Himself; it's the call to be on a mission of redemption.

I recently had the privilege of writing a book with Andy Pettitte, star pitcher for the Houston Astros and formerly the New York Yankees. It's entitled *StrikeZone* (Broadman & Holman, 2005) and deals with a man's commitment to guard his character, integrity, and purity. During a book signing at Nashville's Opryland Hotel, a reporter asked Andy, "Do you feel you've been called to the major leagues?" Without a moment's hesitation, Andy responded, "Absolutely. I know that God has placed me there to serve Him and to be *on mission* for Him."

I couldn't help but smile, because I knew my friend really got it! As Andy pitched for the Yankees in the World Series, his goal was not only throwing strikes but also calling attention to the One who

You may see your work as ordinary, but God prepared you for it and placed where you are for a reason.

had given him that great pitching arm. Was it so he could be seen as Mr. Nice Guy, God's pitcher? Heck, no. Andy wanted the pennant as much as any player on the team! It's because Andy wants others to come to know and depend on God as Lord and Savior of their lives—as he does.

You may see your work as ordinary, but God prepared you for it and placed you where you are for a reason. I'll share with you three of the eight principles from a book that I mentioned earlier and co-wrote, *Made to Count*, which fleshes out the process for discovering what to do with your life.

- God calls *you* to partner with Him in a mission that is bigger than you are.
- God calls *you* to be *on mission* with Him right where you are—starting now.
- God will repeatedly bring *you* to a crossroads of choice as He forges you for His mission.

God's Expectations for Your Performance

God wants you and me to make a difference in our world, to be "salt" that flavors this world with the grace of God and "light" that shines into the darkness, illuminating Him as the ultimate answer to life (Matthew 5:13–14). Do you wonder how those expectations apply to your life on the job? Try asking yourself some important questions.

Who's your boss? Does your workplace have performance evaluations? Probably so. As Christians, we're held to a higher standard than just pleasing our boss, the union, the company president, or our board of directors. In Colossians 3:23, God challenges us concerning our work: "Whatever you do, work at it with all your heart, as working for the Lord, not for men." God is saying that Christians above all others are accountable to Him for how they do their work. If Christ is making a difference in us, it should be obvious to our co-workers. They should see our focus, our priorities, our commitment, our team efforts, our productivity, and our results.

In Genesis, Joseph illustrated his commitment to his real Boss when he served as the estate manager for Potiphar. When Potiphar's wife attempted to seduce him, Joseph's immediate response was, "How then could I do such a wicked thing and sin against God?" (Genesis 39:9). Isn't it interesting that he didn't say "sin against Potiphar"? Joseph knew his ultimate source of authority was the Lord.

How do you serve? In today's workplace, so much of our motivation is to obtain position, prominence, power, possessions, and promotion. But Jesus had a radically different perspective: "Whoever wants to become great among you must be your servant and whoever wants to be first must be your slave—just as the Son of Man did not come to be served, but to serve, and to give his life as a ransom for many" (Matthew 20:26–28).

Do you go beyond expectations in your service at work? When was the last time you asked what else you could do when you finished your project? Are you doing everything possible to make your supervisor or team or company successful? Do you understand that it's not about *you* at work; it's about reflecting the One you serve?

What do you share? Jesus's last words to His followers before ascending into heaven were that He would empower them to be witnesses for Him. Witnesses are people who truthfully and clearly report what they have seen or experienced. For Jesus's followers, this meant communicating from a firsthand perspective how He had changed their lives and could change the lives of their listeners as well. And, as we've noted, His handpicked followers were not priests or prophets. So obviously they didn't need years of training or volumes of knowledge to minister to others or to see their environment as a mission field. And neither should we.

But being *on mission* does not mean running around and throwing tracts at everyone at work; that's not what you're hired to do! You're hired to fulfill the responsibilities of your job and to do it with excellence. When the opportunity arises and someone "asks you a reason for the hope that is in you" (1 Peter 3:15 NKJV), you

Are you doing everything possible to make your supervisor or team or company successful?

need to be prepared to succinctly and clearly point that person to Jesus Christ.

Are you above the ordinary? Paul challenges us in Colossians 3:16–17 to make sure that the Word of God is deeply engrained in our lives. When the Owner's Manual is part of our DNA, it inevitably works its way out into our everyday lives.

Excellence speaks for itself. Your work results should be among the best in your organization or company. People should be able to look to you as a trendsetter in excellence, going above and beyond the call of duty on a regular basis. They should notice that you care about your team more than your individual work, that you believe nobody's work is done until everybody's work is done.

Steve Hyland is a guy like that. He understands who his Boss is. Steve strives to be different in how he serves. He's always well prepared in what to say when a door opens to witness about his faith, and as an employee he goes above and beyond the call of duty. That's why he's been able to lead from the middle of the pack in a middle-management position at Coca-Cola Corporation, where he's also launched a Bible study. And it's not doing badly either. It ranges from fifty attendees when corporate travel is at its peak, up to four hundred for special events. And Steve's colleagues above and below him on the organizational chart speak highly of him as a worker and leader. He's known as a team player, admired for his integrity, and respected for his high performance.

Billy Graham has said, "I believe one of the next great moves of God is going to be through believers in the workplace." For that vision to become reality, Christ followers can't leave their faith in the parking lot when they show up for work each morning...they have to carry it inside. Don't be willing to settle simply for a career, but instead discover and celebrate the vocational calling God has for *you*.[8]

THE AWAKENING EXPERIENCE PROCESS

phase 3: preparation

My Work Battle Plan

Do you have a sense of hope about your work? Did Dr. Reccord's insight from his own life journey and from other godly men in the marketplace give you a different perspective about working *on mission*? After all, work is the place we spend most of our waking hours in our lifetime. Consider the fact that if you worked forty hours a week until age sixty-five, then you would spend 45 percent of your waking hours in the workplace. Tack on an increase of 5.5 percent for each additional five hours worked each week.

Hours Worked per Week	% of Contributable Hours Spent at Work[9]
40	45%
45	51%
50	56%
55	62%
60	67%

* Assumes 12 hours per day applied to all spheres of life. See endnote for details.

So much time spent at work. Is this a curse? Is work just a necessary evil that we must adjust to, live with, and endure until we can retire and then really experience life? Or could there be greater meaning and purpose in the day-in, day-out regimen of work and life? After reading Dr. Reccord's chapter, the answer is a resounding yes!

Statistics reveal that few people in today's modern world have any degree of satisfaction from their work. A recent *Wall Street Journal* survey reveals an 80 percent dissatisfaction rate among the general workplace population. Only 50 percent of executives are satisfied with their work. Does it have to be this way? No! As Dr. Reccord stated, all of us can have "an intentional and deliberate

> You can now invest your time and energy where you currently work with a newfound purpose.

lifestyle of serving God with excellence and introducing others to Him as [we] go about [our] work."

As you read this, you may be in your zone at work; in other words, you are *on mission*. You may feel that your work taps into your core talents and that you are expanding God's kingdom as you engage life and relate to others in your workplace. Our statistics say that you are among the 20 percent of men who are satisfied with their career.

The other 80 percent of men reading this, if the statistics mentioned above are accurate, do not feel this way. For you, work is drudgery, a necessary evil in life, and you don't see a higher purpose in it. Perhaps Dr. Reccord has jolted your thinking and perspective about your work, and you can now invest your time and energy where you currently work with a newfound purpose.

Or you may be at a vocational crossroads in your life journey. You may feel that it is time to move on from your current job, hear from God, and discover a workplace scenario that taps into your heart and passions. Remember J. T. Williams, one of the Bob's three examples in his chapter? J. T. thought he should go to seminary, but his pastor helped him tap into his real passions for work and life. He ended up in the marketplace and has left an imprint for God on it. If you are at a juncture like this, then utilize all that you have discovered in the Awakening Experience Process to help you pursue work that aligns with what God has written on your heart, aligns with your core talents and passions, and is consistent with your life journey discoveries.

Use the following vocational worksheet to help you sort through your vocational options. The following instructions and the completed example illustrate how to use this tool:

• List your current job options in the "Job Options" column.

• Use a scale of 1 to 5 for each awakening discovery tool applied to a specific job option. The number "1" is a very low rating, and "5" is a very high rating. For example, in the completed vocational

worksheet, this fictional man rated his heart a "1" in his current position. But he rated the opportunity to start a new company with George and Frank a "4." This means that when he looked at the "My Heart" awakening tool, he felt that his current work scenario was far from what God had written on his heart, and the opportunity with George and Frank was very close to his heart.

• Highlight any of the deal breakers in your ratings. Note in the example that the low heart ratings in this man's current position and in the management position at Excel Industries were deal breakers for him. Other deal breakers might include a bad corporate culture, a salary that would not support your family, or unethical leadership.

• Now tally the scores for each job option. The high score would rate as your number one job option. But be careful with these ratings. (After all, even the college football BCS rating system has its flaws!) This tool is not designed to eliminate God's voice, calling, and desires for you. Rather, it is designed to help you filter any workplace options through the awakening discovery tools and gain an objective perspective on your options. Obviously, if you have a strong sense of God calling you to a workplace, then go! (His pull would eliminate the need for this tool.) Many times, however, we have several seemingly good opportunities. This tool is designed to help you filter through them and prayerfully make a decision.

Our statistics say that you are among the 20 percent of men who are satisfied with their career.

Vocational Worksheet
(for those going through a work transition)

Category	Job Options	Alignment with Awakening Discoveries (Rate 1-5 with 1 low, 5 high; Highlight Deal Breakers)				Deal Breakers		Ranking
		My Heart	My Life Story	My Giftedness	Core Values	Corporate Culture	Other?	

Vocational Worksheet ►Fictional Example
(for those going through a work transition)

Category	Job Options	Alignment with Awakening Discoveries (Rate 1-5 with 1 low, 5 high; Highlight Deal Breakers)				Deal Breakers		Ranking
		My Heart	My Life Story	My Giftedness	Core Values	Corporate Culture	Other?	
Staying in My Current Field of Expertise	Management Position at Excel Industries	1	3	4	2	X		Heart is not here
	To start a company with George and Frank	4	4	4	4			#1 (16)
	Stay in my current position and company	1	2	3	2			Heart is not here
	VP position at Post Bio Tech	3	3	4	3	X		Culture is not good!
Farming	Cash out and buy land in Montana	4	1	2	4			#3 (11)
Missions	Full-time missions in the Dominican Republic	5	3	2	4			#2 (14)

How did your vocational analysis work out? Did you gain some objective clarity? Remember, the vocational worksheet is not designed to eliminate your need to hear from God. Rather, if there is any truth from God's perspective in the awakening tools from Phases 1 and 2, then the vocational worksheet should validate what you already know and are learning about yourself. Use this tool wisely, and allow others who know you and love you to interpret and apply it.

Now it is time to think and plan strategically and tactically about how we will exemplify excellence in our work, real concern for people, and a preparedness to share our life story (and God's role in it) to those who inquire about the way we think, live, and relate. By now, you have developed battle plans for your personal life and home life. It is time to do the same for your work life. You will use the same battle-plan process for your work life that you used with your personal life and home life. So there is not a need to explain all the details of the process again. (If you need a reminder on how to use the battle-plan tool, then reread the instructions in the last chapter.)

Again, use the completed example to help you think creatively and guide you toward an application that is unique to you. Don't forget to review your Work Life Awakening Assessment Tool from chapter 1 and all your discoveries in Phases 1 and 2 that apply to your work life, including your guiding convictions relevant to your vocation.

Be encouraged. You are crafting a battle plan for your work front. The enemy of your heart does not like you to pray, reflect, think, and plan this way. You are awakening to how God created you and how He desires for you to live. It's an entirely new way of strategically investing your time and energy in what you do and whom you affect through your work. So ask God how He wants you to live and relate at work—and enjoy the adventure and process! Don't forget to encourage each other to do the same.

Remember, we will integrate and review all of your battle plans at the end of the process, including a time analysis. Don't worry about your projected time for now.

my work battle plan

Awakening to God's Adventure for Me

Family Life Goals	Current Status? (1-3)	Action Steps	By?	Projected Time per Month	Notes
1.					
2.					
3.					
4.					
5.					

Total Hours per Month

my work battle plan ➤ Fictional Example
Awakening to God's Adventure for Me

	Work Life Goals	Current Status? (1-3)	Action Steps	By?	Projected Time per Month	Notes
1.	Intentionally target and pour my life into the young managers in my company.	(2) 👎	a. Approach Denzel and Jerry about this.	4/15	N/A	We all golf anyway. Let's see if we can do it with a purpose to get real about life and see where it goes.
			b. Use our common interest in golf to connect and engage life.	5/1	8	
2.	No longer work on weekends.	(3) ☝	a. Let my management team know why I am doing this.	5/15	N/A	I've been communicating the wrong thing by working weekends. My family has suffered. I don't need to do this. I want to limit my work hours to 50 a week.
			b. Let Susie, my secretary, know and ask her to help me schedule this way.	5/15	N/A	
3.	Upgrade communications and celebration events with my company's staff.	(1) ☝	a. Keep doing what I'm doing, but ask for my staff's feedback and new, creative ideas.	Ongoing	N/A	My staff needs to know that I appreciate them and reward hard work.
4.	Learn to tell my life story, how it connects to God's epic story, and pray for and embrace moments to share it with my staff and clients.	(3) ☝	a. Ask Bob to help me clarify and write my life story in a simple, real way.	6/1	6	I want to be able to tell my story with courage and simplicity, not with an agenda to impose on others.
			b. Pray for God to open up opportunities with those I relate to through my work.	Ongoing	N/A	

Total Hours per Month	**217**

checkup

Time for a checkup. How are you progressing? How did your work
battle plan go? How are you doing in the Awakening Experience
Process? You are advancing. Are you helping your friends do the
same? Are you letting others who love you and know you into your
thinking and planning?

You are now discovering how you can invest your time and energy
to fulfill your life purpose, vision, and mission. You are learning to
apply your giftedness and heart to real people in real spheres in your
life. By now you have completed your personal, home, and work
battle plans. You are in Phase 3 of the Awakening Experience Process—preparing for how you can live the awakened life.

The Awakening Experience Process

Phase 1 **AWARENESS** *Awakening to Who I Am*	Phase 2 **FOCUS** *Awakening to God's Adventure for Me*	Phase 3 **PREPARATION** *Awakening to How I Must Live*	Phase 4 **FREEDOM** *Living the Awakened Life*
My Life in Christ **Taking Inventory** **My Heart** **My Life Story** **My Giftedness**	**My Life Purpose** **My Life Vision** **My Life Mission** **The Primary Obstacles in My Path**	**My Guiding Convictions** **Personal Battle Plan** **Home Battle Plan** ***Work Battle Plan*** Church Battle Plan Community Battle Plan	Friendship Battle Plan Guides Along the Way Time Analysis Life Journey Reviews
Where Am I Now?	Where Does God Want to Take Me?	How Must I Live to Get There?	How Will I Stay the Course?

Your battle plans are meant to give you a sense of how you will engage the enemy of your heart in the different spheres of your life. But, as with any conflict, there are surprises in battles. Unexpected and unpredictable things happen that we cannot foresee. Consequently, you will need to adjust and update your battle plans to take these realities into account. You may download the awakening tools at **www.promisekeepers.org/AwakeningExperience** and keep them in a useable format in your computer or with fresh printouts.

In the next chapter, Erwin McManus will help you think about your church life. Hang on. His writing is poignant, and his message will hit you in the gut. God has gifted him as one of the revolutionary leaders in the church-at-large in our world today.

Be encouraged. Stir each other up in your men's group. Keep each other "in the game." You are advancing. You are discovering and creating a plan to live alert and awake to God and the battle. You are forging a life story that is intricately connected to His epic story, and your role in God's story is essential. Take one step at a time. Keep your spiritual senses alert to God's thinking and input and guidance. Go in faith... and courage.

Onward!

living the awakened life in your church

Erwin McManus

About ten of us were sitting in a small duplex in south Dallas, looking toward the future possibilities for impacting our community with the gospel. The other nine were still uncertain of my qualifications; I was the new guy on the block. For decades, these faithful few had given their lives to serve their impoverished neighborhood. Facing some of the highest crime and murder rates in the country, their task was made all the more difficult.

This was my first official pastorate, and at fifty dollars a week, I was certainly overpaid. As I overviewed our assumed-to-be minimal assets, I suddenly discovered that we had more than twenty thousand dollars in the bank! Not bad for a handful of people ministering to a community predominantly on welfare. I soon learned that this money was from the gifts of generous believers who supported our work. When I insisted that we use the funds to reach the city rather than to maintain a financial net for the church, one of the men in the meeting frantically declared, "But we must survive!"

I will never forget the look on their faces when I promised that I would either lead us to impact the city or—in the effort—close our doors. I was a very young believer at the time and only in my twenties, but I was sure there was no promise in the Bible that ensured survival. Once survival has become our supreme goal, we have lost our way.

The New Testament word for *witness* is the same as for *martyr*. We have come to know martyrs as those who have died for the faith. They didn't survive, but they died facing the right direction.

Around the world, Christian families, tribes, and communities have been persecuted and brutally killed for their faith. They didn't survive, yet they left a witness. The purpose of the church cannot be to survive or even to thrive, but to serve. And sometimes servants die in the serving.

The life of the church is the heart of God. The heart of God is to serve a broken world. When Jesus wrapped a towel around His waist, He reminded us that only He could wash away our sin. The church cannot live when the heart of God is not beating within her. God's heartbeat is to seek and save that which is lost. The church exists to serve as the body of Christ, and it is through this commitment to serve that our engagement to culture is secured.

The serving that we are called to requires direct contact. You cannot wash the feet of a dirty world if you refuse to touch it. There is a sense of mystery to this, but it is in serving that the church finds her strength. When she ceases to serve the world around her, she begins to atrophy. In pathology, atrophy is the wasting or decreasing in size of any part of a body. When the church refuses to serve the world, she begins to waste away. She finds herself deteriorating, withering, and losing her strength. Like a muscle that has been locked away in a cast, the church shows the signs of atrophy that become evident when the cast is removed. It is difficult to ignore the reality that the church has lost significant muscle tissue. All around us, we find evidence that the church of Jesus Christ in our contemporary society is not what she once was.

The Great Awakening

Some claim that it was on June 17, 1963, that the end began. That was the day prayer was removed from public schools. Christians argued about this date as if everything was fine on Tuesday and then fell apart on Wednesday. Certainly I am not saying that this was not a sad day for followers of Christ; but this assessment is not only naive, it is indicative of our disconnection to the real crisis. The

It might be fair to say that we lost the power to transform culture.

crisis did not begin when prayer was removed from public schools but when we stopped praying. This event was not the starting place of our cultural decline but the result of years of the church's diminishing influence on society.

Many people have described this as a cultural war, and often our view seems rooted in a perspective that is a battle of the churched against the unchurched. Whether it is in the arena of political perspectives or government policy, we tend to speak about the shift from a Christian worldview as if it were instigated and implemented by those who were outside of the church's reach.

Our language communicates a deep cultural chasm that assumes tremendous distance between the conflicting parties. But if we look more closely at what is really happening, we will be even more disturbed. Very little distance remains between those who we feel affirm Christian values and those who seem committed to the elimination of those values from the American conscience. From athlete to actor, musician to politician, both those who advocate the heart of God and those who seem to war against Him have many times been the product of the Western church. The problem has not been that these individuals of significant influence were outside of the sphere of the church's influence but that, in fact, they sat in the center of the church and remained unchanged at the core.

America's best atheists are children of the church. It is rare to find a person who is a passionate enemy of the church who has never had contact with her. The diminishing influence of the American church on American society is not simply because fewer people are going to church, but fewer people are going to church because of the diminishing influence of Christ on the church itself.

The church, at best, fell asleep. It might be fair to say that we lost the power to transform culture. We accommodated to a culture that was for us user-friendly. We equated being a good citizen with being a good Christian. We lived without persecution and soon found ourselves without conviction. We didn't lose America; we gave her away! In our panic and powerlessness, we turned to political means to seek to regain what we once had through spiritual awakening. Yet even as a moral majority, we could not accomplish what God could through Gideon's few volunteers.

Clearly the world around us was shifting. What we couldn't figure out was why it seemed so disconnected from the influence of the Christian faith. Christianity had become a world religion. It carried all the trappings that came with that distinction. The church was no longer the shaper of modern culture, but modern culture had become the shaper the church.

This should be our great awakening. The world changed, and we didn't. The world changed for the worse because we didn't change at all. The world changed for the better, and we missed the exchange. The world waits for the church to once again become God's agents of change.

The Bible Community Fellowship Church

"We're looking for a church that meets our needs." It seems like I've heard this one a thousand times. The phenomenon of church shoppers has profoundly shaped the contemporary church. The entire conversation is not about relevance but convenience. The focus is not in serving the world; the church itself became the focal point. Our motto degenerated from "We are the church, here to serve a lost and broken world" to "What does the church have to offer me?" This move has made the pastor the only minister, while making the members the only recipients of ministry. What is lost in this process is an army of healers touching the planet.

In many ways, the emergence of the suburbs and the realities of "white flight" paved the way for the community church. After World War II, we experienced growing prosperity and peace. The suburbs were born out of the postwar 1950s. They served as our shelter from the problems in the world. We lived in this intersection between rural values and urban conveniences. During the next twenty years,

> The church became a refuge from the world rather than a force in the world.

the suburbs also became the urban refuge. While our cities experienced urban decay and our society began to destabilize, we were able to hide outside the center.

Massive and sprawling planned communities were created wherever baby boomers wanted to colonize. Understandably, these communities could be characterized by a few emerging and identifiable patterns: homogenous, educated, and white-collar. These suburbs birthed the community church, which is—in itself—a good thing. Starting churches everywhere they are needed is always important. Yet at the same time, we can attribute much of our present dilemma to the role that the community church has played. The portrayal of the church as a fortress became a prevailing value. The church became a refuge from the world rather than a force in the world. Predictability and stability became dominant themes. The cultural environment became comfortable, and the gospel shifted from a church *on mission* to a church that supported missions.

Another aspect of our culture that emerged from this era was the concept of customer service. We both expect and demand to be treated as consumers. "If you want our patronage, you had better cater to my needs." This type of ideology became a reality for the church. In both traditional and contemporary churches, the member became the customer to whom the product was tailored.

He walked confidently up to me on a Sunday morning. It was clear he knew his way around a church. He kind of stood out since he was wearing a suit and tie; our cultural apparel is much more casual than that. He introduced himself and explained that he had been attending for a little over a month. He informed me that the teaching met his standards, the music was acceptable, and he was pleased with what he found in the children's and youth ministries. He went on to explain that he was married and had several children. When I asked him where they were, he explained that they were not yet allowed to attend. He wanted to check us out for several weeks before he brought his family. He wanted to make sure the products and services were in line with what he felt his family needed. This wasn't about theology; this was all about customer service.

Unfortunately, this is the case for too many people. We've been taught that we are the center of the universe, and we evaluate everything on its ability to meet our needs. Some of the best communicators of the Scriptures I know have had people leave their churches for the express reason that they're not being fed. I know that we are the sheep of God and sheep require the Shepherd to feed them, but there must come a time when we become shepherds who feed others.

Is it really all about us being fed? I think it might be important to remember that more than 60 percent of Americans are overweight or even obese. Is it possible this is also true in the arena of personal spirituality? Are we too much about us getting fed and too little about us exercising our faith?

Too many of our statements about the crisis in the American church center on the superficial arena of style and neglect to go to the core issue of self. At the core of so much of the resistance the church is experiencing is the preservation of selfishness and self-centeredness. It is one thing to have a preference; it is another to demand that one's preferences be honored above the needs of those without Christ.

Safe Theology

Out of the community church context has come an unending parade of pop and bumper-sticker theologies—the kinds that give us comfort for all the wrong reasons. One of these in particular has both misguided the church and diluted the calling on every believer who is shaped by it. You've heard it said, "The safest place to be is in the center of God's will." I am sure this promise was well intended, but it is neither true nor innocuous. When we believe that God's purpose, intention, or promise is that we will be safe from harm, we are utterly disconnected from the movement and power of God.

Are we too much about us getting fed and too little about us exercising our faith?

I remember sitting in the home of a pastor and his wife just after they'd finished seminary. They were tremendously gifted and had chosen to serve in a small community of a few thousand residents. We began to talk about their future, and I suggested they move to a major metropolitan center, like Los Angeles. I was stunned not so much by their response but by the rationale behind it. With great passion, they told me that God would never expect them to do that. God would never subject their children to the danger and corruption of the city. I remember leaving that night wondering what was happening to the church. If those who prepare for leadership are looking for the safe places, who will lead the church into the dangerous places?

Somehow we have missed the reality of the biblical experience. From Abraham to Paul, those who followed God were subjected to great dangers. Paul describes his journey with Jesus as anything but safe.

In 2 Corinthians 11:23–28, Paul writes:

Are they servants of Christ? (I am out of my mind to talk like this.) I am more. I have worked much harder, been in prison more frequently, been flogged more severely, and been exposed to death again and again. Five times I received from the Jews the forty lashes minus one. Three times I was beaten with rods, once I was stoned, three times I was shipwrecked, I spent a night and a day in the open sea, I have been constantly on the move. I have been in danger from rivers, in danger from bandits, in danger from my own countrymen, in danger from Gentiles; in danger in the city, in danger in the country, in danger at sea; and in danger from false brothers. I have labored and toiled and have often gone without sleep; I have known hunger and thirst and have often gone without food; I have been cold and naked. Besides everything else, I face daily the pressure of my concern for all the churches.

The truth of the matter is that the center of God's will is not a safe place but the most dangerous place in the world! God fears nothing and no one! God moves with intentionality and power. To live outside of God's will puts us in danger; to live in His will makes us dangerous.

How could we ever think the Christian faith would be safe when its central metaphor is an instrument of death? It is not a coincidence that baptism is a water grave depicting death and resurrection. It is no less significant that the ongoing ordinance of the Lord's Supper is a reminder of sacrifice. How did we ever develop a safe theology from such a dangerous faith?

The Perfect Storm

So much has been written on the changing canvas of society. Certainly generational and cultural shifts are significant and need to be addressed. Yet it is my conviction that these are not the essential reasons for the loss of momentum and the atrophy of the church. These rapid and dramatic changes have made for rough sailing these last fifty years; but they are not sinking the boat. There is no perfect storm out there that can sink the church of Jesus Christ. No matter how much or how rapidly culture changes, the church is designed to prevail. Yet with each culture shift, it is painfully obvious that the church has become an institution rather than a movement.

The distinction lies in the fact that institutions preserve culture while movements create culture. Many times, those who attempt to preserve a dissipating culture will also join it in its ignoble demise. Everything about your culture may be born and rooted in the work of the Holy Spirit. But the Spirit of God moves like the wind, leaving a still silence where He once blew and beckoning us to where He now stirs. The church must raise her sails and move with the Spirit, if we are not to be left behind. It is not enough to simply hang on; we must boldly move forward.

The center of God's will is not a safe place but the most dangerous place in the world!

In the end, the crisis is always spiritual. Admittedly, radical changes outside the church demand an even more radical sacrifice from within the church. We understand this when we consider the realities of life for believers in persecuted countries. We champion their sacrifice and willingness to stand for Christ, even at the cost of their own lives. Yet we consider laying aside our traditions and cultural preferences as an unreasonable expectation. From my own experiences, I know that the only storm that can sink a church is the one that rages from within.

Just like urban legends, there are church legends: stories of churches splitting over the color of carpet, pastors being fired for baptizing a person of color, emergency business meetings being called including inactive members for the purpose of firing a too-active pastor. I know of a church that fired their pastor after the church grew to more than one thousand in its first year. I also know of a dying congregation that sold their church to a community center so that the new church that had rented their property and had grown to four hundred in just a couple of years could never take over the property. Why? Because the new church didn't fit their theological construct.

Like urban legends, the church legends that haunt our recent history reveal more about us than we perhaps care to know. In the end, atrophy is never simply about style; it is always about the substance of servanthood. It is about a people who are willing to submit to the lordship of Christ no matter what the personal implications.[10]

phase 3: preparation

My Church Battle Plan

Once again, God uses a gifted man, Erwin McManus, operating in his zone of influence and leadership in the church, to speak truth and life into us as followers of Christ. Sometimes you just have to say, "Ouch! That feels good." How many of us have thought that being in the center of God's will was the safest place on earth? Or how many of us have thought that our church existed to meet our needs? Erwin speaks truth, and we thank him for his faithfulness to do so.

Now it is time to develop a battle plan for your church life. This doesn't mean that you are going to war with those in your church! It does mean that men who follow Christ need to serve God's higher purposes connected to His love and purpose for His church on earth; and our local church is the most real expression of that for us. So we need to strategically invest our time, talents, and treasures into our local church, because that is God's heart and because He will use us to reach others when we surrender and serve His purposes through our church.

You have by now developed battle plans for your personal life, home life, and work life. Now it is time to do the same for your church life. You will use the same strategic and tactical awakening tool, so we won't explain all the details of the process again. If you need a reminder on how to use the battle-plan tool, then reread instructions in the "Living the Awakened Life at Home" chapter. Again, use the completed example to help you think creatively and guide you toward application that is unique to you. Don't forget to review your Church Life Awakening Assessment Tool from chapter 1 and all your discoveries in Phases 1 and 2 that apply to your church life, including your guiding convictions relevant to your church life.

> We need to strategically invest our time, talents, and treasures into our local church, because that is God's heart.

Be encouraged. You are crafting a battle plan for your church front. The enemy of your heart does not like you to pray, reflect, think, and plan this way. You are awakening to how God created you and how He desires for you to live. It's an entirely new way of strategically investing your time and energy in what you do and whom you affect at and through your church. So ask God how He wants you to live and relate to your family of faith—and enjoy the adventure and process! Don't forget to encourage each other to do the same.

Remember, we will integrate and review all of your battle plans at the end of the process, including a time analysis. Don't worry about your projected time for now.

my church battle plan
Awakening to God's Adventure for Me

Church Life Goals	Current Status? (1-3)	Action Steps	By?	Projected Time per Month	Notes
1.					
2.					
3.					
4.					
5.					

Total Hours per Month

my church battle plan ➤ Fictional Example
Awakening to God's Adventure for Me

Work Life Goals	Current Status? (1-3)	Action Steps	By?	Projected Time per Month	Notes
1. Start a ministry for young businessmen in my church and connect mentors to protégés.	(3) ☞	a. Meet with Pastor John and tell him my vision and see what I should do.	4/15	1, 1x	I think a team of us could lead this so that the weight of responsibility is shared.
		b. Tell my vision to Sam and Chad.	5/1	1, 1x 6 hrs./mo.	
2. Rally a group of guys to pray for Pastor John every Sunday morning before he preaches.	(3) ☞	a. Talk to Pastor John about this.	5/15	30 min.	John needs our encouragement. I've felt compelled to do this for some time.
		b. Rally the men in my circle of influence to call out the men to do this every Sunday morning.	5/15	1 x N/A	
3. Stay involved in our small group with Lauren and continue to share life honestly with the other couples.	(1) ☞	a. Keep doing this.	Ongoing	4	These other couples have become family to us.
		Total Hours per Month		**36**	Includes church on Sunday and our small group

checkup

Time for a checkup. How are you progressing? How did your church battle plan go? How are you doing in the Awakening Experience Process? You are advancing. Are you helping your friends do the same? Are you letting others who love you and know you into your thinking and planning?

You are now discovering how you can invest your time and energy to fulfill your life purpose, vision, and mission. You are learning to apply your giftedness and heart to real people in real spheres in your life. By now you have completed your personal, home, work, and church battle plans. You are in Phase 3 in the Awakening Experience Process—preparing for how you can live the awakened life.

The Awakening Experience Process

Phase 1 **AWARENESS** *Awakening to Who I Am*	Phase 2 **FOCUS** *Awakening to God's Adventure for Me*	Phase 3 **PREPARATION** *Awakening to How I Must Live*	Phase 4 **FREEDOM** *Living the Awakened Life*
My Life in Christ Taking Inventory My Heart My Life Story My Giftedness	My Life Purpose My Life Vision My Life Mission The Primary Obstacles in My Path	My Guiding Convictions Personal Battle Plan Home Battle Plan Work Battle Plan *Church Battle Plan* Community Battle Plan	Friendship Battle Plan Guides Along the Way Time Analysis Life Journey Reviews
Where Am I Now?	Where Does God Want to Take Me?	How Must I Live to Get There?	How Will I Stay the Course?

Your battle plans are meant to give you a sense of how you will engage the enemy of your life and heart in the different spheres of your life. But, as with any conflict, there are surprises in battles. Unexpected and unpredictable things happen that we could not foresee. Consequently, you will need to adjust and update your battle plans to take these realities into account. Please download the awakening tools at **www.promisekeepers.org/AwakeningExperience** and keep them in a useable format in your computer or with fresh printouts.

In the next chapter, Greg Stier will help you think about your community life. You may be thinking that you don't have time left for your community. Hang on. Greg may just give you a new way to look at your community. You could be surprised where he goes with it.

Be encouraged. Stir each other up in your men's group. Keep each other "in the game." You are advancing. You are discovering and creating a plan to live alert and awake to God and the battle. You are forging a life story that is intricately connected to His epic story, and your role in God's story is essential. Take one step at a time. Keep your spiritual senses alert to God's thinking and input and guidance. Go in faith...and courage.

Onward!

living the awakened life in your community

Greg Stier

A battle is raging for your community. It is unseen and, therefore, underestimated. Think of it as an invisible terrorist attack in the neighborhood where you live. Satan, the ultimate guerilla fighter, is leading the assault on your community through his network of dangerous demons, the underworld's version of al Qaeda. This invisible battle produces very visible results: broken lives, shattered marriages, skyrocketing suicide rates, escalating drug use, and dysfunctional communities. Sometimes it's hard to see the soul of your community behind all the well-manicured lawns. But if you could if you could see it, you would be shocked.

Jesus saw past all of the invisible walls people hide behind. He saw the very heart of His community. What did He see? The Bible tells us in Matthew 9:36, "When he saw the crowds, he had compassion on them, because they were harassed and helpless, like sheep without a shepherd."

When Jesus looked at His Jewish neighbors, He saw something that His fellow disciples did not see. He saw their brokenness, their sin, their despair, and the assault on their souls. He saw that the devil himself was harassing their souls and that these poor people were helpless against his attacks. But Jesus was not content just to see the problem. He did something about it. He reached out and touched them. He healed them physically, emotionally, and spiritually.

Jesus has a habit of touching the deepest needs of hurting people. His heart for humanity started in the Garden of Eden when God sculptured a man from a puddle of mud. He then put His mouth onto the nose of this makeshift mud-man and "breathed into his nostrils the breath of life" (Genesis 2:7). Jesus handcrafted Adam, the first man, Himself!

Now fast-forward your thinking several millennia to the Incarnation—Jesus touched people once again. He reached out to touch lepers in spite of the dangers of the contagious disease. He touched the blind, the lame, the deaf, and the hurting; and He healed them inside and out. Did you know that of the thirty-nine times the word *touch* is mentioned in the New Testament, twenty-nine refer to Jesus's touching someone during His ministry on earth? We serve a God who touches!

Before Jesus ascended into the heavens, He gave His disciples this *touchy* directive: "But you will receive power when the Holy Spirit comes on you; and you will be my witnesses in Jerusalem, and in all Judea and Samaria, and to the ends of the earth" (Acts 1:8). From this directive, Jesus challenges us to reach out and touch people within our three communities.

Inside Our "People Zone"

When Jesus told His disciples to be witnesses in Jerusalem, He was referring to their most immediate sphere of influence—the communities where they were living. Jesus wanted His followers to start touching others right where they were.

A big part of our Jerusalem, our personal people zone, is our neighbors. These are the men and women, boys and girls God has placed around us and our family so that we can have an impact on them!

What kind of impact? Jesus tells us that He wants us to be "witnesses" to them. How? With our life and our lips! And it takes both. We must *live* the gospel and *give* the gospel.

How well have you done this in your own community? When was the last time you helped a neighbor shovel his walk or clean out his garage? Do you even know your neighbors' names? Have

Jesus wanted His followers to start touching others right where they were.

you ever brought up the gospel with the people living around you? Does your next-door neighbor even know you are a Christian? Are you on the lookout for opportunities to serve your neighbors? When's the last time you actually did? Are you living the awakened life in your neighborhood?

If we want to be Jesus's disciples, we need to learn to reach out and touch others where they live—just like He did. To do so, we'll need to break cultural taboos and kneel down in the mud, so to speak, to get our hands dirty—just as Jesus did. I'm thinking about more than just hugs, handshakes, shoveling the walk, and small talk. I'm thinking about reaching out to the deepest needs of those in your people zone, your immediate community, with the love of God and the gospel of Jesus Christ.

Our immediate community is only the first zone that we're to influence with our faith and allegiance to Jesus.

Outside Our "Comfort Zone"

In Jesus's Jewish world, the Samaritans were despised by the Israelites. The Jews viewed them as half-breed traitors, less than dogs. That's why Jesus stunned His disciples when He asked a Samaritan woman for a cup of water in John 4. When they saw Jesus (a Jewish rabbi) engaging this woman (a Samaritan floozy) in intimate conversation, they were shocked. That just didn't happen in that day. But Jesus reached out to this woman and touched her heart, quenched her thirst, and saved her soul.

So when Jesus tells His disciples in Acts 1:8 to cross the tracks and reach outside their comfort zones, their minds flashed back to the dramatic event at the well. They knew exactly what He was asking them to do . . . and it was uncomfortable for them.

It is no less comfortable for us in today's culture.

As president of Dare 2 Share Ministries, I travel the nation, training Christian teenagers to share their faith inside and outside their comfort zones. In January 2005, we conducted a conference in Columbus,

Ohio, and equipped thousands of teenagers to share the gospel.

And here's the kicker. Right next door to our conference, there was an Anime convention going on at the same time. Anime is like cartoons on steroids. This style of animation started in Japan and has quickly gathered a following of disciples across the world. Movies like *Kill Bill* and cable channels like the Cartoon Network have popularized Anime for adults and children alike.

More than any other demographic, this style of animation appeals to an underground generation of alternative teenagers. Thousands of devoted followers gather at conventions and dress like their favorite characters. Many wear spikes, carry fake swords, and look kind of dangerous.

Some of the Anime teenagers were upset that the convention center in Columbus booked our Christian convention the same weekend as theirs. All the Southern Baptist, Methodist, Lutheran, and Assembly of God teenagers had to pass by the hundreds of costumed Anime devotees on their way to our event. Imagine the angry Animes and the petrified Christians together in the same convention center at the same time. I couldn't have planned it better! What a huge opportunity to take sometimes sheltered Christian teenagers and help them reach out to those around them with the love of Jesus Christ.

The problem was, this wasn't happening at first. On Friday night, many of the Christian teens were whispering jokes to their friends about the costumed Anime fans. As a result, a few small verbal altercations ensued, and the tension was growing.

That's when God did something unbelievable. He raised up a man of God to reach outside his comfort zone. I heard his story through this e-mail from one of the Anime attendees a few days after the conference:

He raised up a man of God to reach outside his comfort zone.

Dear Mr Stier:

My name is Nick. I am 17 and I was an attendee at the Anime convention. I have to tell you when I arrived at the Anime convention and found myself being stared at by a bunch of Christian kids I became very angry. I attend Anime conventions to get away from the type of kids that your conventions attract. I used to attend church and youth group but I walked away from all that 3 years ago when I decided I didn't want anything to do with Christian people who judge and look down on anyone that is not like them. . . .

Not only am I really into Anime, I am also gay.

But God got my attention on Saturday afternoon at the convention when I was talking on the phone to a friend of mine from home. I found out a very close friend of mine had committed suicide on Friday night while I was at the convention. I began to completely fall apart and started to think about just ending my life.

Right then this guy comes up to me and asks if I am okay. We began to talk and I told him what I had just found out, regarding my friend. His eyes filled with tears and he told me he was so sorry and next thing I know . . . this guy, who I don't even know, was hugging me. . . . He just began to pray for me and he later asked if he could take me to lunch. I told this guy all about me. I was thinking since he was a youth pastor, he was going to start telling me how being gay is a sin and how I needed to change my life. I kept waiting for this guy to treat me like the kids had when I arrived at the convention, but he seemed to not be bothered by my white face and outrageous costume and my openly gay lifestyle. I ended up going to lunch with him and he told me about how God had radically changed his life and how a number of years ago he was very close to ending his life.

Anyway to make a long story short, I just knew that God

had sent this guy into my life at the very moment I was thinking about ending my life. I actually began to wonder if he was real or some angel or something, the way he talked to me and listened to me, even with my bad language. It just didn't seem to bother him. He saw through all the walls I was trying to hide behind.

As we walked back to the convention center this guy... asked me if he could pray for me. For the first time in years I was open to God. He prayed and then I prayed and asked the Lord to come back into my life. Suddenly I felt different and I felt like the pain I had been feeling for the past three years was gone! I can't tell you that I have instantly become straight but I have decided to begin to look at my life and why I have chosen the gay lifestyle and why I am always so angry and tormented in my soul....

I have begun to walk with God again because for the first time I met someone who actually seemed to live the life of Christ and not just talk about it. Thanks for teaching people and kids what it really means to be like Jesus.

Sincerely,

Nick

This youth leader, who took the time to reach outside his comfort zone to a weird-looking, weeping kid on a pay phone, is my hero. He is the kind of man who lives an awakened life, aware of his surroundings and sensitive to the opportunities to impact those whom God brings across his path.

He is the kind of awakened man I'm thinking about and asking you to become. How? By starting to reach out and listen and talk with people you wouldn't normally think twice about relating to. Cross socioeconomic, age, racial, and religious boundaries with a question or a comment. If you see somebody crying on a pay phone, ask him if you can help. You could save a life and a soul.

> In the economy of God, every person on this planet is a neighbor.

Across Our "Time Zone"

Who is your neighbor? Who lives in your community? It's broader than you may think. In the economy of God, every person on this planet is a neighbor. What does that mean for you and me if we are to live an awakened life?

It means that we live alert to the global community and serve and engage it in some way. Maybe this means that you and your family sponsor a Compassion International child or two or three. Perhaps it means that you support missions by giving or going, praying or paying. Some of you have international business connections or extended family in a different country whom you need to reach out and touch with the love of Jesus. There are all sorts of ways to be an awakened man in your global neighborhood. Try talking to the missions leader at your church and see how you and your family can get involved outside your time zone.

The Battle Is Raging

The battles in your immediate, extended, and global communities are between the armies of darkness and the body of Christ (see Ephesians 6:12). It is not a war that will be won through political action, neighborhood cleanups, or moral reformation. This war will be won when the men of God lead the way with the love of God and the gospel of Christ, reaching out to hurting people as Jesus demonstrated and commanded us.

What kind of men are these? Jesus described them in Matthew 11:12: "From the days of John the Baptist until now, the kingdom of heaven has been forcefully advancing, and forceful men lay hold of it." Jesus is looking for a few good men—spiritual marines, if you will—to advance the kingdom of God in their neighborhoods and in their world.

Will you be one of them?

THE AWAKENING EXPERIENCE PROCESS

phase 3: preparation

My Community Battle Plan

The war is all around us, isn't it? We've learned throughout this awakening process that this is an epic war. The war is within us, in our homes, workplaces, in our churches, and in our communities. That's because wherever there are people, there is a battle for their hearts and souls. Greg has helped us understand this war and see it in new and real ways. He's also helped us understand the message that Jesus demonstrated and commissioned us with as His followers. He's asking us to change the way we think, live, and relate to hurting people in our communities.

There's no magic formula. It's just a matter of learning to relate to normal people in our everyday worlds and to honestly and freely share the story of Christ in our own lives. We do our part, and God does His part. We "witness" to God in our lives, and His Spirit uses that witness to change other peoples' hearts and souls.

But to do so, we need to think strategically and tactically about how we will invest in and engage people in our community. We're learning that God wants us to live alert and awake to the life He's given us and to the lives He's placed in our path and community. So it's time to develop your community battle plan.

We will use the same format that we used for your other battle plans. By now, you're learning to transfer all of your awakening discoveries into very real action plans. Use the completed example to spark creativity and action for how you will live the awakened life in your community. As with the other battle plans, don't forget to review your Community Life Awakening Assessment Tool from chapter 1 and all your discoveries in Phases 1 and 2 that apply to your community life.

> Wherever there are people, there is a battle for their hearts and souls.

Be encouraged. You are crafting a battle plan for your community. The enemy of your heart does not like for you to pray, reflect, think, and plan this way. You are awakening to how God created you and how He desires for you to live. It's an entirely new way of strategically investing your time and energy in things and people. So ask God how He wants you to live and relate to those inside your people zone, outside your comfort zone, and across your time zone—just as Greg prompted you to. Don't forget to encourage those in your men's group to do the same.

Remember, we will integrate and review all of your battle plans at the end of the process, including a time analysis. Don't worry about your projected time for now. Ask God what He wants you to do, listen for His voice, and plan strategically what He is prompting in you.

Community Life Goals	Current Status? (1-3)	Action Steps	By?	Projected Time per Month	Notes
1.					
2.					
3.					
4.					
5.					

Total Hours per Month

my community battle plan ►Fictional Example
Awakening to God's Adventure for Me

Community Life Goals	Current Status? (1-3)	Action Steps	By?	Projected Time per Month	Notes
1. Learn the names of all my neighbors, begin to pray for them, and ask God to help me be attentive and responsive to their real life needs.	(2) 👎	a. Draw an imaginary square around my house and get to know all eight families around our house.	4/15	N/A	We have barbecues anyway. Why not have a neighbor over once a month?
		b. Invite the Valdezes over for a barbecue this month.	5/1	3	Talk to Lauren about this.
2. Strategically get to know the families of the boys I coach on Conner's soccer team.	(2) 👎	a. Have a barbecue for the entire team.	5/15	6	Four of my players do not have dads in their lives. This will stretch me out of my comfort zone.
		b. Target the fatherless boys on our team and pray about how I can help their family in any way.	Ongoing	N/A	
3. Take a mission trip once every two years with our entire family to a third world country.	(1) 👍	a. We're going to Haiti this year with three other families from church.	Done	A 10-day event	These experiences are really impacting our kids. I want to keep this going.
		b. Think about our next targeted area.			

Total Hours per Month	9	This really doesn't add nine hours to my life, since we eat anyway and I am already coaching soccer.

checkup

How are you doing in the Awakening Experience Process? You are advancing. Are you helping your friends do the same? Are you letting others who love you and know you into your thinking and planning?

You are now discovering how you can invest your time and energy to fulfill your life purpose, vision, and mission. You are learning to apply your giftedness and heart to real people in real spheres in your life. By now you have completed the battle plans in Phase 3. Congratulations! You are moving forward—strategically and intentionally, aligned with the man God made you to be and what His vision and purpose is for your life.

The Awakening Experience Process

Phase 1 **AWARENESS** *Awakening to Who I Am*	Phase 2 **FOCUS** *Awakening to God's Adventure for Me*	Phase 3 **PREPARATION** *Awakening to How I Must Live*	Phase 4 **FREEDOM** *Living the Awakened Life*
My Life in Christ Taking Inventory My Heart My Life Story My Giftedness	My Life Purpose My Life Vision My Life Mission The Primary Obstacles in My Path	My Guiding Convictions Personal Battle Plan Home Battle Plan Work Battle Plan Church Battle Plan *Community Battle Plan*	Friendship Battle Plan Guides Along the Way Time Analysis Life Journey Reviews
Where Am I Now?	Where Does God Want to Take Me?	How Must I Live to Get There?	How Will I Stay the Course?

Your battle plans are meant to give you a sense of how you will engage the enemy of your life and heart in the different spheres of your life. But, as with any conflict, there are surprises in battles. Unexpected and unpredictable things happen that we cannot foresee. Consequently, you will need to adjust and update your battle plans to take these realities into account. Please download the awakening tools at **www.promisekeepers.org/AwakeningExperience** and keep them in a useable format in your computer or with fresh printouts.

In the next chapter, Dr. Tom Fortson will help you think about how you are going to stay the course for the awakened life that you have mapped out. Plans do not self-execute—not in your business, not in politics, not in your church, and certainly not in your life. We have to work the plan. We need other people in our lives to help us do so. Dr. Fortson is going to stir your thinking in this area.

We will also be performing a time analysis on all of your battle plans to see if you actually have the time and space in your life to live what you have targeted to do. This is a process. Don't forget that. One step at a time—headed down the path God wants you to venture.

Be encouraged. Stir each other up in your men's group. Keep each other "in the game." You are advancing. You are discovering and creating a plan to live alert and awake to God and the battle. You are forging a life story that is intricately connected to His epic story, and your role in God's story is essential. Keep your spiritual senses alert to God's thinking and input and guidance. Go in faith… and courage.

Onward!

living fully awake

Thomas S. Fortson, PhD

Not too long ago, my doctor performed a medical procedure on me that required light sedation. The nurse assisting in the process asked me if I wanted to watch the procedure on the TV monitor. I was up for it and thought it would be both interesting and educational. They positioned me on the medical table with the TV monitor situated so I could watch. I'm not sure how much time passed before I asked, "Well, when are you going to turn on the monitor?"

The nurse said, "Oh, we're finished."

Finished! I thought, still in a daze. They had "put me under," as they say. It wasn't deeply under—just a light anesthesia so I wouldn't know what was going on. I was fascinated and thought about all the activity and conversations that had gone on during this procedure while I was in a silent slumber.

This experience prompted me to contemplate how easy it is to live life in a lightly sedated state of existence and miss out on significant activities taking place in my marriage, family, church, and community—and for me to be completely oblivious to what is *really* happening. Do you know what I mean? I wonder how many of us are unaware that our wives don't feel our love. I wonder how many of our children feel disconnected and ignored by us because we are in a lightly sedated slumber produced by an overloaded schedule. I wonder how many people in our churches and communities are hurting, and we don't know it.

We Need Help

I'm not trying to impose some kind of false guilt on you. Although I may be in a different season of life and may be facing challenges different from yours, I know how easy it is to become consumed with my own challenges and be unaware of the needs of my family. Bottom line: I know I need help to live the awakened life, and I'm guessing that, by now, you know it too. I need God's help, and I need the encouragement of others who love Him and love me. Why do I feel this way?

My dad passed away a few years ago. I would love to have asked him more in-depth questions about his life, disappointments, pains, and unrealized dreams. I would probably discover why many of my own needs, unmet as a young boy, still affect me today. We didn't have a lot of material things growing up, and what little we had was the result of Dad's working two and sometimes three jobs.

I was very active in sports during this period, but because of Dad's work schedule he couldn't attend many of my activities. I remember as if it were yesterday one Little League baseball game that he attended. I was up to bat, and the count was three balls and two strikes. I know coaches say that a walk is as good as a hit, but that's not necessarily true when your dad's in the stands. I took a wild swing at the next ball, which was clearly outside the strike zone. To my surprise, I hit it over the right-field fence. I think it was the only home run I hit all season. As I was rounding second base on my way to third, I saw my dad jumping up and down, yelling, "That's my son! That's my son!" One insight you need to know about my dad is that he was not very expressive. I don't remember if we won the game, but I couldn't wait for the ride home with him.

To my surprise, Dad didn't mention the home run. I knew he was proud of me, and I never doubted his love; I just needed to feel and hear it. He expressed it through his excitement to all the other parents nearby. But why hadn't he expressed his feelings to me?

Bottom line: I know I need help to live the awakened life, and I'm guessing that, by now, you know it too.

As a twelve-year-old, I needed to feel his love and affirmation. I was devastated. I remember asking my mom why Dad hadn't told me he was proud of me and expressed it like he did with the other adults. Mom, as usual, just gave me a loving look and said, "Your dad told me what you did and said how proud he was of you."

But why didn't Dad tell me himself? Was he not alert to my emotional needs? I believe he was. He just didn't know how to express it to me. You see, he didn't have a father during his formative years. My granddad was killed in a car accident when Dad was young, and it had a tremendous emotional impact on him. It is only now as an adult, and as I interact with other men, that I realize the tremendous need and emptiness my dad had growing up, longing for the love and physical touch of his father. I only wish I knew then what I know now.

My wife, Toni, often tells me, "You're a chip off the old block." What she means is that I am just like my dad. That's good; I'm proud to be his son. But like him, I had needs in my own family that I sometimes failed to see because I was not alert to them. I wish I could go back, but I can't. What I didn't realize was that Dad had needs in his life that were not met. He needed affirmation, recognition, and approval from his father. I find this experience even more insightful now, because I am more alert and awakened to this need in other men.

We Can Have Hope

I don't think I need to convince you that these are turbulent times in our world. Governments and ideologies continue to collide. Anger and rage prompt illogical suicide bombings and murders. We are confronted daily with the meaningless loss of life. We continually encounter the brokenness of marriages and families and the reality of disease and other tragedies.

Truly, life is an adventure—and a battle—filled with unpredictable surprises that challenge us daily. As president and CEO of

Promise Keepers, I am challenged by my own and others' expectations of me. I face pressure between work demands and the needs of my family. At times, like all of us, I feel overwhelmed and anxious. The enemy knows how to come at me, and at times he blindsides me, causing me to question what I know to be true about God and myself.

I am also challenged by the reality of the state of men in our country—and around the world. One doesn't have to look hard to conclude that the American man today is confused. Consider how the media inundates us with images that portray men as either weaklings or as predators to be feared; while at the same time, society bemoans the loss of strong, godly, "real men." In our culture, it's easy for our career goals to contend with our desire to be loving husbands and good fathers. With all of the demands and pressures, it's easy to isolate ourselves from deep and abiding friendships. Sometimes it just seems safer to retreat into our work or other diversions in order to avoid the deeper issues that tax our souls. We have all heard deathbed regrets of men who realized their feelings of loneliness and isolation at the end of their lives. Eventually, we face the reality that financial, recreational, or sexual pursuits do not satisfy our deepest spiritual needs.

Despite what some consider a gloomy forecast in today's world and despite the challenges, I have hope! I have hope because I've learned in my own life journey that God is faithful. I know the outcome of the epic battle between God's kingdom and Satan's. And I'm learning that I have a role in His eternal purposes—just as you do. I have hope that even though millions of men are living sedated lives, God is awakening millions more to discover their unique purposes for our generation. I have hope because I know the power of my God to change my own life, and I know His power to change a man's heart. I believe "the eyes of the LORD range throughout the earth to strengthen those whose hearts are fully committed to him" (2 Chronicles 16:9). From a human perspective, the times—and

It's too easy to invest our best energy in the wrong things.

men—might appear troubled and bleak. But from God's perspective, there is hope and optimism and anticipation of great things to come.

That is why I'm excited about *The Awakening Experience*. It's too easy to live decades of life without deeply contemplating why we are alive and for what purpose we exist. It's too easy for us as men to be on top of our work game and sacrifice critical relationships in the process. It's too easy to invest our best energy in the wrong things.

The Awakening Experience Process is designed to guide us toward the heart of our heavenly Father and to help us connect with Him. It's a process to help us become clear about whom He has created us to be and what He has created us to do. It's a process to help us optimize our life purpose and discover our role in God's unfolding plan. That's why I have hope.

A Contagious Force

Dream with me for a minute. Imagine that what you have been experiencing through the awakening process with a few friends becomes a contagious spiritual virus that infects other men in your circle of influence. What if those in your work world—your marketplace—become intrigued by the changes they see in the way you think, live, and relate? If you are married and have children, what if your family begins to see changes in you that emanate from something deep in your heart and soul? What if others begin to ask you about the growing sense of focus and peace they observe in you? What if others see how you are strategically investing your time in pursuing God's plan for you?

Do you see where I'm going with this? I believe that when a man discovers why God created him and for what purpose he exists, then that man becomes contagious for God's kingdom on earth.

Think about the potential impact in our churches, communities, marketplaces, and world at large if God transforms a man's heart to follow Christ wherever He guides him. There's a spiritual contagion in this thinking: one man infecting another; and he, in turn, infecting a few others with truth, grace, love, and hope. This vision—men transformed worldwide—fuels me and gives me courage and hope for my time on earth and for the future of Promise Keepers.

Men Sharpening Men

If you have engaged the lives of a few other men in this Awakening Experience Process, then you know each other more deeply and authentically than when you began. Few things in this life compare to the gift of safe, close friends and brothers in Christ who love God and encourage each other to attain their potential. Few things are more powerful than men who are alert and awakened to their life purpose and who have a plan to fulfill it. Men like this are a spiritual force with which the enemy must reckon.

I was recently reminded of something C. S. Lewis once said. In his essay "The Weight of Glory," Lewis described the Christian's awareness of eternity as "a load so heavy that only humility can bear it."[11] In the same way, leading Promise Keepers is a responsibility I can face only with utmost humility.

I do know that God has prepared me for this time. Indeed, I cannot imagine a better mentor, or coach, than Bill McCartney, cofounder and former president of Promise Keepers. We worked together side by side for years—Coach on the field and I in the press box, as he liked to say—guiding the present and future of this ministry. As executive vice president and chief operations officer for a number of years at Promise Keepers, I became familiar with the inner workings of this ministry. But more than this, because I worked so closely with Coach Mac, I witnessed firsthand what it means to be an awakened, fully alert man after God's heart. Coach Mac exemplified for me a man of vision—a man humble in heart and hungry for God. It is in this spirit that I am committed to use my God-given talents, gifts, and life experiences, to follow and expand the vision to see men spiritually transformed worldwide.

Proverbs 27:17 says, "As iron sharpens iron, so one man

Few things are more powerful than men who are alert and awakened to their life purpose sharpens another." That is what Coach Mac has done for me. God used him to sharpen me spiritually, to help me understand the awakened life in Christ, and to equip me to lead with a sense of alertness. God desires the same for all men who follow Him. He has put this ability to sharpen one another in all of us. That's why we need each other to live the spiritually awakened life. That's why Promise Keepers designed the Awakening Experience Process as one through which men progress *together*.

Now that you have written an awakening plan, you will need other godly men to encourage you and help you *live* the awakened life. You will need other men to help you follow through and practice what you know to be true about who you are, what you must do, and what you will become in your lifetime. That is why Promise 2 of the Seven Promises of a Promise Keeper states: "A Promise Keeper is committed to pursuing vital relationships with a few other men, understanding that he needs brothers to help him keep his promises." Men who are clear about who they are and how they must live can help each other fulfill God's purpose for their generation.

Freed to Serve in Love

Paul writes in Galatians 5:13–14, "You, my brothers, were called to be free. But do not use your freedom to indulge the sinful nature; rather, serve one another in love. The entire law is summed up in a single command: 'Love your neighbor as yourself.'" As you complete the Awakening Experience Process and think and plan about how you will now live the awakened life, I want to leave you with three words: *freedom, service,* and *love*—the three core words in this passage.

Freedom

Freedom is a compelling concept in our world these days. Even now, we see seeds of freedom blossoming in the Middle East. Who would have thought that Afghanistan, Iraq, and the Palestinians would honor and facilitate free, democratic elections? Who would have thought that Lebanon would, en masse, publicly demand free elections? It is true: a desire for freedom is branded on the human heart.

But more than political or social freedoms, the human heart longs for authentic spiritual freedom. As other authors in this book have eloquently communicated, only Christ frees our hearts from dark traps and vices and heals us from human brokenness. A freed heart is a heart God can use. A heart set free by Jesus Christ is able to accomplish what Christ requests of it. A freed heart lives a life alert to and aware of all the activity going on around it.

However, there is a warning in Galatians 5:13 for a freed heart: "But do not use your freedom to indulge the sinful nature." The battle that rages within us as followers of Christ is best fought when we satisfy our desires and hunger for God. Feed the spiritual desires of your spiritual heart in Christ, and the sinful desires of the flesh will diminish. You will actually begin to crave the things of God more than the things of your sinful nature. When that happens, you are in the zone of real spiritual freedom.

> Love must motivate all that we do and become.

Service

Ironically, real spiritual freedom grows when we give our lives away in service to others. Life is ultimately about relationships. When Christ awakens us to our purpose in life, we begin to experience the joy and freedom of responding to Him by serving others. As we serve, we become God's vehicle for introducing others to Him. Our actions bring life to our words and convictions. Our battle plan, developed in earlier chapters, inherently targets how each of us can live as a vessel or instrument in service to God and to others. Our ability to progressively serve others is critical to living the spiritually free and awakened life. That is why Paul says, "You, my brothers, were called to be free. But do not use your freedom to indulge the sinful nature; rather, *serve one another* in love" (Galatians 5:13; emphasis added). A freed man is free to serve others. Let us use our freedom and our awakening plan to serve at home, at work, at church, and in the community.

Love

Paul then says, "Serve one another *in love*" (Galatians 5:13; emphasis added). It is possible for you and me to serve our wife, children, friends, or those in our workplace, and to do so without love. It is possible to serve begrudgingly and with an unloving edge to our service. Love is so central to God's heart and the entire Bible that Paul said, "The entire law is summed up in a single command: 'Love your neighbor as yourself'" (v. 14). Love must motivate all that we do and become.

As you near the completion of the Awakening Experience Process, infuse all of your thinking and planning with freedom that is motivated to serve others . . . in love. If you grow in this, and I grow in this, then this kind of spiritual freedom will spread. It's contagious.

Living the Awakened Life

My son, Tommy, is a pilot. He has earned his instrument and commercial ratings. Through the years, I've learned to trust his training and piloting skills. Others have asked, "Are you nervous when you fly with your son?" My answer is simply, "No." That's because I trust the process whereby he became a licensed pilot.
I trust his skills with the plane and the instruments.

Bad weather or high winds can easily cause you to get off course and become lost. I once asked him while flying, "Hey, Tommy, what happens if we get lost?"

"Oh, that's easy, Dad," he stated. "There are four steps we follow: climb, call, confess, and comply." You *climb* to gain altitude and a better perspective of the situation. You *call* air-traffic control, which monitors all aircraft in the air. You identify your aircraft type, tail number, current heading, altitude, and destination. You *confess* that you are unable to make out your present location. When the pilot acknowledges he is lost, the tower will then request that he squawk a transponder code, which is a series of numbers that enables them to identify the aircraft on radar. This gives air-traffic control a clear picture of where the aircraft is. Finally, you *comply*. You follow the vectors, such as heading and altitude, that the controller gives you to get back on course.

Learning to live an awakened life and being alert to the needs around you is similar to flight training. If you get off course, you can get back on course with some needed help. Tommy has progressed through an extensive training process to attain his present level of skill and confidence. It is similar with us as men learning to live the awakened life.

In *The Awakening Experience*, we have each gone through a process to gain clarity. Each of us has learned to focus our energy and life on the things that matter in our personal life, home life, work life, church life, and community life. Each of us now has a plan. It is time to implement this plan of living the awakened life. As we do, let's remember Galatians 5:13: "You, my brothers, were called to be free. But do not use your freedom to indulge the sinful nature; rather, serve one another in love."

> It is time to implement this plan of living the awakened life.

phase 4: freedom

My Friendship Battle Plan

Are you gaining insight into what it means to live alert and fully awake to the life God created you to live? Dr. Fortson used the illustration of his sedation while undergoing a medical test. How often does it seem that life just zips by us while we're still waiting to watch the monitor, only to discover we missed the view? The fact is: life is fast. Time does fly. We are here on earth for a relatively short time, and so we want to awaken to God's design and desires for us so that we can optimize the time we do have.

You may recall that the featured verse in the introduction of *The Awakening Experience* was Romans 13:11, in which Paul says: "And do this, understanding the present time. The hour has come for you to wake up from your slumber, because our salvation is nearer now than when we first believed." Through the Awakening Experience Process, you have awakened from your slumber and are more alert to how you can live with understanding and embrace the life of salvation God has freely given you.

Perhaps by now you are tired of the word *process*. Fair enough. Substitute the word *progression* or the phrases *one step at a time* or *a systematic course of action*. You get the point. No matter what you call it, we have simply been applying basic strategic thinking and planning principles to our lives.

Before we complete this awakening process, it is worth asking the question: What does God think about planning our lives? Is He for it, against it, or ambivalent toward it? These are credible questions.

Listen to what God thinks about what we have been doing. "To man belongs the plans of the heart, but from the LORD comes the reply of the tongue. All a man's ways seem innocent to him, but motives are weighed by the LORD. Commit to the LORD whatever you do, and your plans will succeed" (Proverbs 16:1–3). God does care about us living a strategic, awakened life. He is neither removed nor unresponsive to this process. He is watching how we plan our lives, and He is listening and looking for something specific as we plan.

God is looking at our motives as we develop our awakening plan. He is weighing the posture and drive of our hearts. Are we crafting self-serving plans that feed self-indulgent drives? Or are we designing plans that honor Him, expand His kingdom, and serve His eternal purposes? If *self* drives our planning, then we are on our own; it's as if God's judgment is, "Okay, then. I will not bless your plans. I will not walk with you. You will not have My support to live your awakening plan." If we are driven by the latter, then God says, "Commit to [Me] whatever you do, and your plans will succeed." Once again, it's about our heart—what drives us, what motivates and energizes us, and whether our heart is free and surrendered to courageously pursue and live the life God made us to live.

Right now, people are making plans of all kinds. That's because the God who created us is a planner, and we are made in His image. Thus Proverbs 16:1 says, "To man belongs the plans of the heart." We all inherently plan. Some plans are God-honoring and bring value to life and humanity. Other plans are evil, destructive, and crafted in dark places. Governments plan. Businesses plan. Engineers plan. Teachers plan. Terrorists plan. Get the picture? The question is: what is the motive behind the planning?

You have progressed through three phases of a four-phase process we are calling the Awakening Experience Process. Assuming that you have asked God what He thinks about your planning up to this point and have listened and responded to Him, then you currently have a plan that is motivated to honor God with the life He has given you. You have discovered how He has designed you. You have tapped into what He has written on your heart. You have highlighted critical discoveries from your life story. You have identified your unique

An isolated man is an easy target for the enemy.

giftedness. You have written your life purpose, vision, and mission statements. And you have created five battle plans, one each for your personal life, home life, work life, church life, and community life.

How will you now begin to live the life God has awakened in you?

Let's first state the obvious—*plans do not self-execute!* Many great strategic plans sit lonely in three-ring notebooks on dusty shelves and will never be implemented. It's one thing to think and plan strategically. It's quite another thing to actually implement a plan and change the way and manner in which people do things.

It's the same way with our plan to live an awakened life. Consequently, we need a *map* to implement our awakening plan.

At the core of our awakening implementation plan is the pursuit and connectedness to a few fellow journeyers, or comrades in arms, who also intend to live an awakened life. Ecclesiastes 4:12 says, "Though one may be overpowered, two can defend themselves. A cord of three strands is not quickly broken." We fight the war in God's epic story most effectively when we are authentically connected to Him and a few other men. We cannot live the awakened life alone. We can try, but eventually we'll discover that we need help. We need God's help, and we need the help of a few close buddies who love God and who love us. As Dr. Fortson said, that is why Promise Keepers is committed to encouraging men to acknowledge their need for brothers-in-Christ to help them keep their promises (Promise 2). An isolated man is an easy target for the enemy. But if you have a few close comrades in your life, you are a dangerous force and threat against darkness.

As a result, the next thing we need to do in our awakening process is craft a battle plan for our friendships. Like anything in our lives, if we don't strategically carve out time and space for these relationships, they will not develop; so we need to make time to invest in—and be encouraged by—a few real, authentic friends.

In the introduction you were encouraged to experience the Awakening Experience Process with a few other men—to get real and to cover each other's lives, confessions, and hearts as you engaged life on a deeper level. If you actually did this, then you and your buddies have connected meaningfully. Most likely you will want to continue your awakening group and gather strategically for regular checkups, encouragements, insight, and prayer. Or you may want to pursue some other men, guide them through the Awakening Experience Process, and transmit the spiritual virus, as Dr. Fortson alluded to.

Whichever route you choose, you will need a few other men in your life who know you thoroughly, who have the freedom to relate to you honestly, and who believe in the life God has created you to live. Together, you will encourage each other, help each maneuver through the unpredictable realities of life, and pray for one another.

In the table below, list the names of your fellow journeyers who are core friends for your awakening adventure:

My Core Friends	1.
	2.
	3.

As you identify your core friends, understand that over time they will read your awakening plan, and you will read theirs. You will guide them through your plan, and they will guide you through theirs. They will most likely probe and question your plan and in doing so sharpen your thinking. You will do the same for them. Together, you will give each other freedom to encourage each other, challenge each other, and help one another actually live the awakened life.

You should meet regularly with your comrades in arms—at least once a month. When you get together, bring your awakening plans with you and encourage each other to move towards the "thumbs-up" status in your battle-plan goals. Give each other grace . . . and truth. "Consider how [you] may spur one another on toward love and good deeds . . . [and] encourage one another—and all the more as you see the Day approaching" (Hebrews 10:24–25). These are your comrades in arms, your fellow journeyers in the battle of life who are committed to live the life God created them to live.

For those of you who are married, consider how you will communicate and invite your wife into a full awareness of your awakening plan. Spiritually, you are one with her; so you will want to move toward oneness in allowing her fully into your thinking and planning. For many of you, this is not a problem and not an issue. For others, you may need guidance from other men, depending on the issues you are facing in your marriage. Be wise. Listen for God's guidance and leadership on how to introduce your wife to your discoveries. Ideally, she has been involved in the awakening process with you. But if she hasn't, it might be too much for her to absorb if she has a low-risk, fearful-of-change personality. You may need your friends' help on this one. But over time, you want to move toward complete openness, transparency, and freedom with your wife. Just be wise on how you get there.

phase 4: freedom

Guides Along the Way

In addition to our friends (and our wife, if we are married), we need guides at strategic times in our life journey. Some of us need a guide or coach in the area of being a loving and encouraging husband. Some of us need a guide in the area of fathering. Some of us need a spiritual guide. Or a business guide. Or a career guide. Or a missions guide. You get the picture. Our life guides are in our life for a short period of time. For example, you may need a marriage mentor in your life for two or three years. In the space below, identify the life guides you need now and the sphere of life for which you need help. If you have actual names of men to pursue, write them down. If you know the sphere of life where you need a guide but don't know who, then leave the name space blank. You may want to ask your friends for their suggestions and pray for God to help you find specific life guide.

My Life Guides	Sphere of Life
1.	
2.	
3.	
4.	
5.	
6.	

Now it is time to develop your friendship battle plan. You have identified your awakening fellow journeyers, your core friends, and needed life guides. Like the other life-sphere battle plans, we need to have an action plan to live the awakened life and to experience the ultimate freedom that Christ has made us to live. We are in Phase 4 of the Awakening Experience Process.

The Awakening Experience Process

Phase 1 **AWARENESS** *Awakening to Who I Am*	Phase 2 **FOCUS** *Awakening to God's Adventure for Me*	Phase 3 **PREPARATION** *Awakening to How I Must Live*	Phase 4 **FREEDOM** *Living the Awakened Life*
My Life in Christ Taking Inventory My Heart My Life Story My Giftedness	My Life Purpose My Life Vision My Life Mission The Primary Obstacles In My Path	My Guiding Convictions Personal Battle Plan Home Battle Plan Work Battle Plan Church Battle Plan Community Battle Plan	*Friendship Battle Plan* *Guides Along the Way* Time Analysis Life Journey Reviews
Where Am I Now?	Where Does God Want to Take Me?	How Must I Live to Get There?	How Will I Stay the Course?

It's now time to think strategically and tactically about how we will invest in and engage our friends and life guides. Remember, we're learning that God wants us to live alert and awake to the life He's given us. To do so, we need help—God's direct help and His help through other people—just like Dr. Fortson explained. So, it's time to develop your friendship battle plan, which includes accountability and encouragement with a few other men and a few strategic life guides.

We will use the same format that we used for the other battle plans. By now, you're learning to transfer all of your awakening discoveries into real-life action steps. Use the completed example to spark your creativity and thinking for how you will live the awakened life alongside some core friends. As with the other battle plans, don't forget to review your friendship inventory assessment from chapter 1 and all your discoveries in Phases 1 and 2 that are relevant to your friendships.

Be encouraged. You are crafting a battle plan for your friendships. The enemy of your heart does not like you to pray, reflect, think, and plan this way. You are awakening to how God created you and how He desires for you to live. It's an entirely new way of strategically investing your time and energy into things and people. So ask God how He wants you to live and relate to your close friends and life guides. Don't forget to encourage those in your men's group to do the same.

Remember, we will integrate and review all of your battle plans in the next step of Phase 4 in our Awakening Experience Process, including a time analysis. Don't worry about your projected time for now. Ask God what He wants you to do, listen for His voice, and plan strategically what He is prompting in you.

my friendship battle plan

Awakening to God's Adventure for Me

Friendship Goals	Current Status? (1-3)	Action Steps	By?	Projected Time per Month	Notes
1.					
2.					
3.					
4.					
5.					

Total Hours per Month

my friendship battle plan ➤ Fictional Example
Awakening to God's Adventure for Me

#	Friendship Goals	Current Status? (1-3)	Action Steps	By?	Projected Time per Month	Notes
1.	Connect deeply and authentically with Steve and Jim, and grow in what it means to encourage each other to live the life God created us to live.	(2) 👎	a. Share my heart with them at our next lunch together.	4/15	6	These guys are safe. I know they care for me and love me and want me to succeed.
			b. Take the risk to open my heart to its depths.	5/1	(2x/mo.)	
2.	Find and relate to a spiritual life guide in order to grow in faith and maturity.	(3) 👉	a. Meet with Pastor John to see if he knows of a good match for where I am and what I need.	5/15	N/A	I need a mature, older man who is real and who can encourage me in some areas that I'm weak in right now.
			b. Talk to Red about where I'm at.	5/15	N/A	
			c. Meet once a month with the mentor.	6/1	2	
			Total Hours per Month		**8**	

phase 4: freedom

All right, give each other a high-five—just like you would at a Promise Keepers conference. You've almost completed your awakening plan. You've gone deep into understanding who you are—in Christ—and the purpose and mission for which God created you. And you've taken this journey with a few other men. It's been an adventure—but it's not over.

Before we address the reality of time and how you will begin to live your awakening plan, ask yourself some important pit-stop questions. Are you gaining clarity? Are you beginning to see your life more from God's perspective? Do you feel more focused now that you have developed battle plans for each sphere of your life? Do you have hope, and a plan, to live more intentionally and more aligned with your Creator?

Time is one commodity on earth that we cannot increase or decrease.

Remember, this is a journey; and the journey doesn't stop now that you are near the end of this awakening process. The journey is ongoing because life is constantly unfolding. But you now have a life map, a written guide to help you transverse the figurative mountain ranges, swamps, deserts, and oceans in your life journey. Though you will need to revisit your awakening plan regularly to adjust and edit it and to refresh your battle-plan goals and action steps, you do have a map to work from.

But before we finish this process, we must address an important reality in our awakening plan: the reality of time, with its limitations and capacity.

You shouldn't be surprised that we are born into space and time. Time is one commodity on earth that we cannot increase or decrease. We all have the same allotment of time, and so we must learn to steward and live within its parameters.

If we don't understand and learn to steward time, then, on one hand, we begin to feel stretched too thin, overcommitted, burned out, and used up. On the other hand, we can feel bored, purposeless, and trapped in no man's land. So we need to perform an honest time analysis on our battle plans. Until now, you have restrained from allowing time to limit your battle-plan thinking. But now it's time to apply brutal honesty to your plans and expectations. To do so, we need to: (1) get real about real-time, (2) know our capacity, (3) prioritize our battle-plan goals, and (4) adjust to the unpredictable changes inherent in the seasons of life.

The Awakening Experience Process

Phase 1 **AWARENESS** *Awakening to Who I Am*	Phase 2 **FOCUS** *Awakening to God's Adventure for Me*	Phase 3 **PREPARATION** *Awakening to How I Must Live*	Phase 4 **FREEDOM** *Living the Awakened Life*
My Life in Christ Taking Inventory My Heart My Life Story My Giftedness	My Life Purpose My Life Vision My Life Mission The Primary Obstacles In My Path	My Guiding Convictions Personal Battle Plan Home Battle Plan Work Battle Plan Church Battle Plan Community Battle Plan	Friendship Battle Plan Guides Along the Way *Time Analysis* Life Journey Reviews
Where Am I Now?	Where Does God Want to Take Me?	How Must I Live to Get There?	How Will I Stay the Course?

Get Real About Real Time

Let's think about the reality of time by calculating some numbers and agreeing upon some basics.

Parameters	Real-Time
Number of Days in One Year	365
Number of Weeks in One Year	52
Number of Months in One Year	12
Number of Weeks in One Month (average)	4.33
Number of Days in One Week	7
Number of Hours in One Day	24
Number of Hours in One Week	168
Number of Hours in One Month	727
Number of Hours in One Year	8,724
Number of Hours in 70 Years	**610,680**

We are asked to steward our lives in such a way that we fulfill our role —within time and space.

It's bizarre, isn't it, to look at life this way? Add to this thinking the fact that we do not know how many years, months, and days God will grant us on earth, this side of heaven. We do know this: God created each one of us for a unique role in His eternal, epic story. For the time we have on earth, we are asked to steward our lives in such a way that we fulfill our role—within time and space.

Preachers often talk about an eternal perspective compared to a temporal one. What does this mean? Hebrews 11:13–16 gives us insight into how we should view our time on earth, however long it is. As you read these verses, capture the internal outlook of how real people in Scripture lived in real time on earth:

These all died in faith, not having received the promises, but having seen them afar off were assured of them, embraced them and confessed that they were strangers and pilgrims on the earth. For those who say such things declare plainly that they seek a homeland. And truly if they had called to mind that country from which they had come out, they might have had opportunity to return. But now they desire a better, that is, a heavenly country. (NKJV, emphasis added)

Real people—like Abel, Noah, Abraham, Sarah, Jacob—lived their years on earth with an internal perspective that their time on earth was connected to a larger, unfolding story: God's eternal and unfolding purposes.

Your life is also connected to a larger, unfolding story. If we were to draw an imaginary time line of God's epic story and place our time on earth within it, it might look like this (understanding that God's time is eternal, infinite, and never-ending):

Our lives on earth are but a dot on the time line of history—an important dot, but just a dot in time. If you live seventy years, you have 610,680 hours *on earth* to fulfill your unique role in God's eternal kingdom on earth. When we think about it, we don't have that much time—within the big-picture of time—to fulfill our role in God's unfolding drama.

So we need to get real about real time. There's no need to panic or to get in a hurry. Rather, we may need to slow down and focus so that we live on purpose and on mission. And that is what you have been doing in *The Awakening Experience*—gaining clarity about how you can live your life on earth and serve God's purposes for your generation. That is why it is not a matter of doing more stuff faster. It is a matter of living within time and space with clarity and focus about why we are alive and for what purpose. To do so we must have a realistic view of time.

Know Your Capacity

We have 8,794 hours each year to live on purpose and pursue our life mission. If you sleep eight hours a night, you will spend 2,920 hours resting your physical body. If you work forty-hours a week for forty-nine weeks (with three weeks of vacation), you'll spend another 1,960 hours working. That leaves 3,914 hours in one year to allocate to your personal, family, church, community, and friends, including drive time for work, chores, and margin to just *be*.

Are you getting the picture? Time is real. You know this. And if we don't steward it, we become fragmented, dispersed, and ineffective. So we need to agree on some basic assumptions about time when we think about living a life awakened to God's epic story and our role in it.

If we break down time to the monthly level, how much time do we really have to implement our battle plans? The table below presents some basic assumptions relevant to helping you live an awakened life:

> We may need to slow down and focus so that we live on purpose and on mission.

Awakening Plan Assumptions	Time
Number of Hours per Day	12
Number of Days per Week	7
Number of Weeks in One Month (average)	4.33
Number of Hours per Month Available for Your Awakening Plan	364

Why twelve hours per day applied to your awakening plan? Where do the other twelve hours go? Well, let's say eight of those twelve hours are applied to a good night's sleep. If you commute thirty minutes one way to work, then you have three hours to shower in the morning, read the newspaper, brush your teeth, cut the lawn, poop-scoop your yard, help your kids with homework, wash the car, fix the sink, watch the nightly news, balance your checkbook—you get the picture.

Now you might decide to apply more than twelve hours per day to your awakening-plan goals. For example, you might say that you only need six or seven hours a night for sleep. Warning: be careful! God may not be asking you to fit more into your life, but He does want you to live on purpose and on mission. So before you adjust the time assumptions of the awakening plan, perform a time analysis of your battle plan using the assumptions just stated. Here's your primary assumption, then, regarding time available for your awakening plan: *364 hours per month.*

As you think about your capacity, start with an honest assessment of how increased work hours affect the rest of your life. The graph below illustrates how adding five hours to a work week squeezes and shrinks the other areas of your awakening plan.

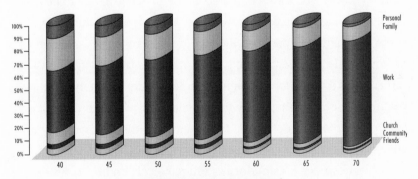

Hours Worked Per Week for One Month

If you work a forty-hour week, you will apply 48 percent of your 364 hours available to live your awakening plan to the work front (figured by multiplying 40 hours x 4.33 weeks per month = 173.2 hours each month ÷ 364 hours = .476 or 48 percent). If you work 42 hours each week you will spend exactly 50 percent of your time at work—the tipping point of spending more than half of your time available for your awakening plan at work. When you add five hours to your workweek, you add (on average) 6 percent to your work front—which means you must take away 6 percent of time you had allotted to other things besides work. When we view time and our capacity this way, it's easy to see why an extended routine of over-working negatively impacts our marriage and family.

Here's the principle: when one area of our life expands, other areas of our life must shrink. Why? Because we cannot add more time to our lives, but we can steward it and live with awareness to our capacity. We all have the same time capacity—364 hours per month available to live the life God created us to live. That is why we need to live awakened to the reality of time and know our capacity. Next, we need to prioritize our battle-plan goals.

Prioritize Your Battle-Plan Goals

A priority is a main concern. A priority supersedes other people and things. By now, you have crafted six battle plans designed to help you live the life God created you to live. We are now at the place in the Awakening Experience Process to perform a time analysis on your battle plans. By doing so, you will discover whether you can actually do all that you planned in 364 hours per month. Your guiding convictions that you wrote in chapter 5 will help you priori-tize your battle-plan goals if your plans exceed the time capacity of 364 hours per month.

As an example, let's perform a time analysis on the six battle plans that our fictional man in the examples illustrated. The table that follows tallies his hours.

On the first chart, our fictional man is close to the capacity of 364 hours per month, but he is still seven hours beyond it. He knows that one of his guiding convictions for his family is not to sacrifice his family for any other sphere of life. So on the second chart he decides to trim seven hours out of his work life. In addition, he realizes that he has not allotted enough time for his kids. Also

Here's the principle: when one area of our life expands, other areas of our life must shrink.

on the second chart he decides to make it a goal to work forty-five hours a week instead of fifty and give the extra time to his kids. In doing so, he shrinks his work life from 217 hours each month to 195 hours a month, and applies 15 more hours each month to his family (remember he was over 7 hours in his first time analysis). His adjusted time analysis (on the second chart) allows him to create a baseline foundation for him to move forward and begin to invest his life in the things God has created him to do and become.

Sphere of Life	Battle-Plan Goals	Projected Time per Month	% of Time per Month
Personal Life	Time with God	27	
	Exercise and Nutrition	26	
	Financial Budgeting and Oversight	5	
	Woodworking	9	
Home Life	Intentional Dating and Time with Lauren	16	
	Monthly Dates with my Kids	6	
Work Life	50-Hours-a-Week Workweeks	217	
Church Life	Ministry to Young Businessmen	6	
	Small Group with Lauren and Sunday Church	22	
Community Life	Monthly Barbeque with a Neighbor	3	
	Coaching Soccer for My kids	20	
Friendships	Time with Steve and Jim	12	
	Time with a Spiritual Mentor	2	
	TOTALS	371	

awakening plan time analysis ►Fictional Example 2

Sphere of Life	Battle-Plan Goals	Projected Time per Month	% of Time per Month
Personal Life	Time with God	27	18%
	Exercise and Nutrition	26	
	Financial Budgeting and Oversight	5	
	Woodworking	9	
Home Life	Intentional Dating and Time with Lauren	16	10%
	Monthly Dates with my Kids	21	
Work Life	45-Hours-a-Week Workweeks	195	54%
Church Life	Ministry to Young Businessmen	6	8%
	Small Group with Lauren and Sunday Church	22	
Community Life	Monthly Barbeque with a Neighbor	3	6%
	Coaching Soccer for My kids	20	
Friendships	Time with Steve and Jim	12	4%
	Time with a Spiritual Mentor	2	
	TOTALS	**364**	**100%**

You may look at this man's time allotment and conclude that he needs to reprioritize some of his goals. And you may be right. But he does have a baseline from which to stay honest and real about time and his own capacity—and to reprioritize his battle-plan goals as God leads him and as he chooses.

Now it's time for you to perform a time analysis on your battle-plan goals. To do so, review your awakening plan discoveries (your heart; giftedness; life journey insights; your life purpose; vision; mission; and guiding convictions). Then reread your six battle plans and fill in the following time analysis tool. If you exceed 364 hours per month, then you will need to make some strategic decisions to live within the reality of time and your capacity. (Remember, you can access **www.promisekeepers.org/AwakeningExperience** and download all of *The Awakening Experience* tools, including the time analysis tool.)

You may also discover that you are not balanced in the way you desire, and you may decide to delete some of your battle-plan goals in order to create more time for your priorities. For example, if you stated in your personal battle plan that you wanted to earn a college degree, and you have three teenagers at home, you may decide to put your educational pursuits on hold until your kids leave home and invest in them for the next several years.

Use the wisdom and perspective of your wife (if you are married) and your friends to help you think objectively and realistically.

> You may need to make some strategic decisions to live within the reality of time and your capacity.

awakening plan time analysis

Sphere of Life	Battle-Plan Goals	Projected Time per Month	% of Time per Month
Personal Life	------- ------- -------		
Home Life	------- ------- -------		
Work Life	------- -------		
Church Life	------- -------		
Community Life	-------		
Friendships	-------		
	TOTALS	364	100%

How did your time analysis go? Are you within the 364-hour limitation? If not, were you able to make the strategic decisions to edit your battle-plan goals within this time capacity? If we are to effectively steward our lives within the time frame God has given us, we must stay real about time, know our capacity, and prioritize our lives and plans accordingly. Next, we need to adjust to the unpredictable changes of life with its unique seasons and surprises.

Adjust to Unpredictable Change

The time-analysis tool will help you to stay honest and to make strategic decisions that come your way in the future. Your life, as you discovered in your life journey graph, has unique chapters and seasons to its unfolding story. If you are a young single man, then you are in a season of life in which you have more time to invest in nonfamily things. But if you are married with kids at home, you are in a season of life in which you must invest more time in your home front and less time in other things. As your kids grow and leave home, you will have more time available for other things that God has prepared for you.

In addition to the unique needs that each season of life inherently contains, we face unpredictable surprises that have the potential to greatly interrupt our thinking and planning. For example, a family tragedy or illness naturally prioritizes family in our lives and puts other things on hold. Or a one-month project at work may require an extended investment of our time; and when we know this and communicate it to our wife, we potentially alleviate long-term tension in our marriage. Other interruptions are not tragic but just as real in their impact on our time. For example, our figurative man in our examples allotted twenty hours a week to coaching his kids' soccer teams. Most likely, this coaching is approximately a two-month investment of time. After the soccer season ends, he will have twenty hours per month to apply to other battle-plan goals.

Do you see how you can steward the time that God has given you

> Do you feel more focused and hopeful now that you have a plan to move forward?

to more effectively fulfill your life purpose and mission within the unique seasons of your life? We cannot predict the future, but we can live in a way that is more aligned with God's purpose for us and strategically steward our investments of time to fulfill His desire for us.

Wrap-Up

You have completed the Awakening Experience Process! You now have a map to move into your future and a plan to work from.

Compare for a minute where you are now to where you were when you started *The Awakening Experience*. You now have insight into who you are. You have written your life purpose, vision, and mission. You have developed guiding convictions that will help you transverse the unpredictable crossroads in your future life journey. And you have developed battle plans for your personal, home, work, church, community, and friendship spheres of life. You have gone through a four-phase process over a period of weeks and months. Do you have more clarity? Do you feel more focused and hopeful now that you have a plan to move forward?

The Awakening Experience Process

Phase 1 AWARENESS Awakening to Who I Am	Phase 2 FOCUS Awakening to God's Adventure for Me	Phase 3 PREPARATION Awakening to How I Must Live	Phase 4 FREEDOM Living the Awakened Life
My Life in Christ Taking Inventory My Heart My Life Story My Giftedness	My Life Purpose My Life Vision My Life Mission The Primary Obstacles in My Path	My Guiding Convictions Personal Battle Plan Home Battle Plan Work Battle Plan Church Battle Plan Community Battle Plan	Friendship Battle Plan Guides Along the Way Time Analysis Life Journey Reviews
Where Am I Now?	Where Does God Want to Take Me?	How Must I Live to Get There?	How Will I Stay the Course?

Now the journey begins!

As you begin to actually experience your awakening plan, realize that this is not about instantly living 100 percent of it. That's just not reality. Look at it this way: if you are living 30 percent of your plan one year from now, then you are further along living on purpose and on mission than you would have been had you not planned anything. What if you are living 50 percent of your awakening plan two years from now? And what if you are living 85 percent of it in five years? Isn't that better than living unfocused, in a slumber, and out of touch with God's design and purpose for your life? Of course it is. So be careful, especially if your personality is an "all-or-nothing" type.

As you begin to live an awakened life, use your friendship battle plan to meet strategically with your comrades in arms, your core friends, and your life guides to evaluate how you are doing. Remember, you will need to plan to meet at least once a month. When you do, pay special attention to the thumbs-sideways and thumbs-up goal status. You should also plan to fully review and edit your awakening plan at least once a year. The week between Christmas and New Year's is a good time to do this.

> "Don't burn out; keep yourselves fueled and aflame."

Make this your annual spiritual (in the same vein of thought of an annual physical). Share your revisions and new insights with your core friends. Overall, learn to help each other move your battle-plan goals into the thumbs-up category. Encourage each other to pursue the life God has called each one of you to live. Take to heart the words of Paul in Romans 12:9–12:

> Love from the center of who you are; don't fake it. Run for dear life from evil; hold on for dear life to good. Be good friends who love deeply; practice playing second fiddle. Don't burn out; keep yourselves fueled and aflame. Be alert servants of the Master, cheerfully expectant. Don't quit in hard times; pray all the harder. (MSG)

Remember, life on earth is a journey and a battle. The enemy of your heart and life is not pleased with your thinking and planning. Be alert to his schemes and tactics in the days ahead. You can bank on the fact that he will attempt to discourage you and thwart your awakened thinking, living, and relating. He will do all he can to derail you from the awakened path you have chosen—all the more reason to be alert and aware to the times in which we live. It's also all the more reason to pray for your buddies and ask them to pray for you.

Cover each other's backs with grace and encouragement. Check up on one another. Listen for His voice. Keep in step with His Spirit (Galatians 5:25). Keep each other on the path God has revealed through this process. And go live the life story that is intricately connected to His epic story. Faithfully fulfill your role in it. Go in faith... and courage. And enjoy the journey.

Onward!

►notes

1. John Eldredge, *Wild at Heart: Discovering the Secret of a Man's Soul* (Nashville: Thomas Nelson, 2001), 85. Used by permission.

2. Getting to the core of your heart is a process that at times feels mysterious or impossible. You may want to read one or more of the following books to stir your thinking and reflection. Larry Crabb, *The Pressure's Off: There's a New Way to Live* (Colorado Springs: Waterbrook Press, 2002). John Eldredge, *Wild at Heart: Discovering the Secret of a Man's Soul* (Nashville: Thomas Nelson, 2001). Erwin Raphael McManus, *Seizing Your Divine Moment: Dare to Live a Life of Adventure* (Nashville: Thomas Nelson, 2003).

3. Carl Henry, as quoted in Edith Draper, *Draper's Book of Quotations for the Christian World* (Carol Stream, IL: Tyndale, 1992), 74.

4. A. W. Tozer, *The Pursuit of God* (Camphill, PA: Christian Publications, 1982), 73.

5. Material from this chapter is adapted from Buddy Owens, *The Way of a Worshiper: Discover the Secret to Friendship with God* (Lake Forrest, CA: Purpose Driven Publishing, 2005). Used by permission.

6. Numerous spiritual-gift discovery resources exist. Your church denomination may have one, or you can search the Internet and find many that guide you through a questionnaire and e-mail you the results. We will not employ these tools in the Awakening Experience Process. That does not mean it would not be helpful for you if you are inclined to pursue and use one of these resources.

7. W. H. Murray, "Until One Is Committed," *The Scottish Himalaya Expedition* (London: J. M. Dent & Sons, Ltd., 1951).

8. Material from this chapter is adapted from Dr. Bob Reccord, *Made to Count: Discovering What to Do with Your Life* (Nashville: W Publishing Group, 2004). *Made to Count* and the companion workbook, *The Made to Count Life Planner* (Nashville: LifeWay Church Resources, 2005), offer eight life-changing biblical principles fleshed out with the stories of believers in all walks of life who are making their life count by fulfilling God's calling right where they are. Used by permission.

9. These figures assume eight hours each night for sleep and four hours each day applied to life issues like driving to and from work, eating, personal hygiene, household chores, and so on. Twelve hours, then, are assumed left to apply to personal, home, work, church, community, and friendships life goals. The percentages in the table represent, then, a twelve-hour-a-day scenario.

Math: 7 days x 12 hours/day x 52 weeks/yr. = 4,368 hours/yr. If a person starts working at age 18 and retires at 65, he/she will have worked 47 yrs. x 4,368 hrs./yr. = 205,296 total hours applied to life goals. Assuming a 3-week vacation each year for 47 years, or 49 weeks/yr. x 47 yrs. = 2,303 total workweeks. That number times the number of hours worked each week divided by 205,296 yields the percentages in the table.

10. Material in this chapter is an adapted excerpt and condensation of Erwin McManus, "Chapter None: Atrophy," *An Unstoppable Force: Daring to Become the Church God Had in Mind* (Loveland, CO: Group, 2001), 22–36. Used by permission.

11. C. S. Lewis, "The Weight of Glory," *The Weight of Glory: And Other Adresses* (New York: HarperCollins, 1949, renewed 1976), 31. Used by permission.

►about the promise keepers authors

Chapter 1 ► Dave Roever

President, Roever and Associates, Fort Worth, Texas, www.daveroever.org

As a naval riverboat gunner in Vietnam, Dave Roever was burned beyond recognition when a grenade exploded in his hand. His survival and life are miraculous.

Today a public speaker, Dave also is a frequent guest on national TV talk shows. Often drawing upon his war experiences of loneliness, peer pressure, disfigurement and pain, as well as life's triumphs, Dave shares a message of courage, commitment, and survival.

Uniquely qualified to speak to the needs of military personnel, Dave regularly addresses domestic as well as deployed troops. He is also active in mission work in Vietnam and other places.

Roever is founder and president of two nonprofit corporations: Roever Evangelistic Association and Roever Educational Assistance Programs. He has authored four books: *Welcome Home, Davey*; *Scarred*; *Nobody's Ever Cried for Me*; and *Magic Fountain*.

Dave and his wife, Brenda, make their home in Fort Worth, Texas. They have two adult children, Matt Roever and Kim Chapin, and four grandchildren.

> This side of death we will always battle against our flesh.
>
> —Harold Velasquez

Chapter 2 ► Harold Velasquez

Vice President of Creative Services, Promise Keepers, Denver, Colorado, www.promisekeepers.org

Harold Velasquez has served as the vice president of Creative Services for Promise Keepers since January 2001. Harold came to Promise Keepers with many years of experience in the music industry, several years in pastoral leadership, and over five years in Christian television. He is the visionary leader who heads the creative team that originates, designs, and implements all the programmatic elements of the Promise Keepers men's conferences. His team also develops many of the small-group resources that equip men for life.

Harold and his wife, Joyce, married since 1974, are the parents of three daughters, Jessica, Erica, and Bianca. Jessica and her husband, Vince, live with their two sons in Dallas. Erica and her husband, Pat, live with their son in Denver.

Chapter 3 ▶ Buddy Owens

Editorial Director, Purpose Driven Publishing, Purpose Driven Ministries, Saddleback Church, Lake Forrest, California, www.purposedriven.com

Buddy Owens is the editorial director of Purpose Driven Publishing and a pastor at Saddleback Church in Lake Forest, California. He is the author of *The Way of a Worshiper: Discover the Secret to Friendship with God* and is the general editor of *The NIV Worship Bible*.

A noted speaker on spiritual formation and the role of worship in a believer's life, Buddy has spoken at over fifty Promise Keepers events over the past seven years.

Before coming to Saddleback, Buddy held the position of vice president at Maranatha! Music for fifteen years. He has also served as a worship and programming consultant for numerous national ministry organizations, including Promise Keepers, Focus on the Family, Billy Graham Evangelistic Association, Harvest Crusades, Luis Palau Evangelistic Association, United States Armed Forces Chaplains' Board, and the Nationally Broadcast Concert of Prayer.

Buddy and his wife, Lynnda, have four children and live in Mission Viejo, California.

Chapter 4 ▶ Reggie Dabbs

Pastor, First Assembly of God Church, Fort Meyers, Florida, www.thesilverdome.org

Reggie Dabbs is the staff evangelist for the First Assembly of God Church in Fort Meyers, Florida.

He began his speaking career after graduation from North

Central Bible College in Minneapolis, Minnesota. Once during a speaking engagement, his host asked if he would interested in addressing a high school assembly. From that small beginning in 1987, Reggie developed a full-time ministry to kids.

Reggie is a popular speaker in the public school system where he talks to kids in a humorous style about choices each kid has when faced with drugs, alcohol, suicide, etc. He is one of the most in-demand speakers who helps teenagers meet their problems head-on and overcome them.

Reggie hosted the Promise Keepers Passage Young Men's event in December of 2001, and he served as the emcee at every PK event during the 2004 season. He will continue to use his gifts to engage and impact the men at each of The Awakening events during the 2005 season.

Chapter 5 ▶ Bishop Joseph L. Garlington, Sr., PhD

Senior Pastor, Covenant Church of Pittsburgh, Pennsylvania, www.ccop.org

Bishop Garlington is the founder and senior pastor of Covenant Church of Pittsburgh, an inner city, multiracial expression of reconciliation and community with a membership of 2,500.

He is the leader of Reconciliation! Ministries International, a network of churches and ministries. He also gives oversight to churches in the United States as well as in other parts of the world. Bishop Garlington travels extensively around the world and is recognized for his ability to bring people into the presence of God through his preaching and singing abilities.

He is the featured worship leader on a Maranatha! Music recording and has also recorded several other worship albums.

Bishop Garlington is the author of *Worship: The Pattern of Things in Heaven* and *Right or Reconciled: God's Heart for Reconciliation!*

Bishop Garlington and his wife, Barbara, have seven children and eleven grandchildren and have seen most of their children join them in the work of the ministry.

A servant attitude will change your home like nothing else can.

—Dan Seaborn

Chapter 6 ▶ Dan Seaborn

Founder, Winning At Home, Zeeland, Michigan, www.winningathome.com

Dan Seaborn is the founder of Winning At Home, Inc., an organization designed to assist and encourage people of all ages and stages of family and marriage. The Winning At Home staff has developed a date night called "Marriage Rendezvous."

As a featured speaker at family conferences, corporate functions, universities, marriage conferences, and at churches of all denominations, Dan is recognized for sharing his passion to develop individuals and families to lead Christ-centered homes.

Dan hosts three daily radio programs, which can be heard on over 450 religious and secular radio stations in the United States and around the world. He has authored seven books on the topic of marriage and family.

Dan formerly pastored in Holland, Michigan, where he started the W.W.J.D. craze with his youth group.

Dan and his wife, Jane, live in West Michigan with their four children.

Chapter 7 ▶ Bob Reccord, PhD

President, North American Mission Board, Alpharetta, Georgia, www.namb.net

Dr. Reccord is the president of the North American Mission Board, the missions agency for the Southern Baptist Convention. It fields approximately 5,200 missionaries across North America and some 2,400 chaplains. In 2004 they facilitated the mobilization of almost 25,000 students in World Changer projects to rebuild substandard housing in inner cities, sharing Christ as they worked. In addition, NAMB serves as the nerve center of one of three largest disaster relief agencies in America. Over 25,000 Southern Baptist Church members have been FEMA-certified from Baptist state conventions across America.

Prior to leading NAMB, Bob was a pastor and served the denomination in leading personal evangelism training and heading up U.S. clinics for Evangelism Explosion.

Dr. Reccord's most recent works include: *Made to Count; The Made to Count Life Planner; Live Your Passion, Tell Your Story, Change Your World* (coauthored with Randy Singer); *Launching Your Kids for Life* (with wife, Cheryl); and *StrikeZone! Pursuing a Life of Purity and Integrity* (with Houston Astros' pitcher Andy Pettitte).

Other published works include: *Beneath the Surface: Steering Clear of the Dangers That Could Leave You Shipwrecked; When Life Is the Pits;* and *Forged by Fire.*

Bob lives in Alpharetta, Georgia, with his wife, Cheryl, an accomplished pianist and speaker. They have three children, Christy, 28, Bryan, 25, and Ashley, 21.

Chapter 8 ▶ Erwin McManus

Pastor, MOSAIC, Los Angeles, California, www.mosaic.org

Erwin McManus serves as lead pastor and cultural architect of Mosaic, a multicultural, multiethnic urban church that meets in various places in the LA area. Mosaic's name comes from the diversity of the members and is symbolic of a broken and fragmented humanity from which God can create a work of beauty.

McManus is a national and international speaker on issues of church growth and organizational change, leadership, postmodern culture, and urban and global issues. He has served as a guest professor and lecturer at numerous seminaries and universities across the United States. He partners with Bethel Seminary as a distinguished lecturer and futurist.

Erwin is also the founder of Awaken, a personal and organizational creativity development group and serves as a contributing editor for *Leadership Journal.*

Erwin and his wife, Kim, have two children, Aaron and Mariah, and a daughter in the Lord, Paty.

> The church must raise her sails and move with the Spirit, if we are not to be left behind.
>
> —Erwin McManus